A DECADE OF
DIAPERS

LEARNING TO PARENT GOD'S WAY:
THROUGH HARDSHIP

LISA D. WEITKAMP

xulon
PRESS

www.xulonpress.com

TABLE OF CONTENTS

Acknowledgments. vii

Introduction. xi

Chapter One 13

Chapter Two 19

Chapter Three 25

Chapter Four 32

Chapter Five 39

Chapter Six 48

Chapter Seven 56

Chapter Eight 63

Chapter Nine 71

Chapter Ten. 79

Chapter Eleven 86

Chapter Twelve 96

Chapter Thirteen 106

Chapter Fourteen. 121

Chapter Fifteen 127

Chapter Sixteen. 134

Chapter Seventeen 143

Chapter Eighteen. 151

Chapter Nineteen 158

Chapter Twenty. 164

Chapter Twenty-One. 174

Chapter Twenty-Two. 182

Chapter Twenty-Three 192

Chapter Twenty-Four 201

Chapter Twenty-Five. 207

Chapter Twenty-Six 213

Conclusion 219

Scriptures for Devotionals and Bible Studies 223

ACKNOWLEDGMENTS

Many people helped me share my story, and I will not take full credit for its success. First and foremost, I have to thank my Father. He gave me the gift of writing and the desire to pursue it. Through other people, He showed me what to say and how to say it.

Tina Barry, thank you for the idea! This is where it all started. I still remember that day when we discussed the prospect of writing a book about my life and you suggested this part of it. That was in 2013. Now look where I am.

Danny, thank you for working so hard to allow me to stay home, which provided me the time I needed to complete this huge endeavor. The title you came up with is just perfect! Your support was unwavering and you were open to sharing your life with others. Let's face it; you are one of the main characters, like it or not.

Hunter, Colt, D.J., and Autumn, thank you for being so forgiving and understanding. Without you, I would never have learned how to show God's love. I wouldn't be the person I am today, nor would I have this story to tell.

Pastor Larry Salings, thank you for your wisdom and spiritual guidance. Through your bold leadership, I discovered my true calling. You allowed me to use it with the congregation so that I could grow in my gift. Your prayers for me have been answered.

Vicky Kaseorg, thank you for your encouragement and inspiration. I watched you be blessed as you followed God's plan to share your stories. I believed I would experience the same outcome if I persevered and I am already seeing the blessings!

Alex McGilvery and Amy Fox, thank you for your time and insight. Thank you for all those red and blue markings on my manuscript which were there only to show me how to enrich my inspirational memoir.

Brianna Boes, thank you for organizing and leading our writer's group, which played a key role in the development of my book as well. It may seem your input was minor, but in reality it led me down the right path. I would not have known which direction to take if you and the other members had not pointed the way.

Jeff Lockett, Lisa Traynor, Nichole Bryant, Mandy Magruder, Frank Chapman, and Gennifer Monteer, thank you for reading the rough copy. Your feedback was the final step before I handed it over to Xulon Press. After you read it, I knew it was time to set my story free. No more holding on.

For the rest of my friends and family who supported me, including my mom (Peggy Kraft), Lareesa Merritt, Beth Yoder, Kendra Windsor, Facebook friends, and all my church family, thank you from the bottom of my heart. I am truly blessed.

Last, but not least, a sincere "Thank you!" goes to you, my readers. Without you, my book would be nothing but a collection of words. I hope my story inspires you and gives you hope. I pray that God speaks to you with His special voice that only you can hear. May He be known to you like never before. May you find your true identity in Him, through hardships and in triumphs. Don't forget Him. He didn't forget you. He is with you always.

May God bless all of you! Happy reading.

INTRODUCTION

T he problem for me was I held the Truth in my head and
not in my heart. It hadn't sunk down deep into my soul,
in spite of growing up attending church, having been saved
at seven, and baptized at ten. I was even re-baptized as a
teenager. Of course I knew the Bible like the back of my
hand, right? Given that I had spent endless hours listening to
Sunday school lessons, sermons, small group Bible studies
and countless years of church camp presentations, it would
be fair to think I had it all together.

Fair, but wrong. No one close to me had encouraged me to
use my faith, or not enough anyway. Rather, it floated on the
surface, being blown around by the world's lies. Lies that told
me I should not ask for help. Lies that told me God could not
be trusted to do what He said He would do. Lies that told me
I could do everything on my own. I even believed the lie that
I had to look and act a certain way to be accepted by others.

Friends were a rare commodity for me. Most of my youth
was spent hiding in my room listening to music, reading

books, and dwelling on whatever worries crossed my mind. Sometimes I thought about marrying and raising my own family. Sometimes? Okay, I admit I might have been a bit obsessed with finding Mr. Right.

As I dreamed about my future, I tried to ignore the one question that lingered in the back of my mind: Could I be a mom, a GOOD mom? I had babysat my neighbor's three rambunctious boys, whom, although I loved dearly, couldn't tolerate to be around for too long before I wanted to go crazy. Maybe having my own kids would be different? But would I be able to handle the messes, the lack of sleep, and constant demands, even for the sake of my own flesh and blood?

Doubts still plagued my mind when I married Danny, my best friend and soul mate. (Marrying at all was a miracle in itself because of my hermit-like lifestyle!) My doubts were magnified even more after I was prescribed Paxil for my panic attacks. I had some fairly big anger issues too. My feelings, left to build up inside of me for too long, turned into raging adult temper tantrums. How could I be a Godly role model for my young and innocent offspring while behaving in such ways? I was sure I could not. A victim mentality is what I had.

When I asked God to change me, I expected Him to change me *before* I had kids. I didn't realize that He had different plans. He used my kids to change me. I never imagined the journey traveled would be to a whole new me. My firstborn, Hunter, arrived February 4th, 2004. A Decade of Diapers had begun!

CHAPTER ONE

FACING THE UGLY TRUTH OF BEING A NEW MOM

"But the wisdom that comes from heaven is first of all pure; then peace-loving, considerate, submissive, full of mercy and good fruit, impartial and sincere."
James 3:17

"Why are you crying?" I yelled at Hunter, my one-week-old son, who I held in my arms. He had been wailing incessantly for thirty minutes and I had tried every trick I knew.

"What is wrong with you?" I pleaded with him.

I faced an ugly truth about myself. My worst fears had come true. I had hoped that sweet, quiet person I appeared to be on the outside would be strong enough to overcome the not-so-pleasant person I was on the inside. This was not the case, though, especially during highly stressful times. I was already on Paxil for anxiety, but it could only do so much. I had not yet undergone the therapy needed to fix the issues tormenting my soul. The antidepressant only covered the symptoms. My doctor had never suggested seeing a therapist, either. In fact, at my request, he repeatedly filled the medication, month after month, year after year.

But back to my story. On this particular night, Danny was working. If he had been there, he would have taken Hunter. He adored his son. While Hunter and I were still in the hospital, Danny would rush to see us after he finished his evening shift as a diesel mechanic.

I couldn't do much with our tiny, newborn son the first few hours after the birth because I was hooked up to IV's for blood pressure, fluids, and antibiotics. I admired Danny for keeping his promise to be an available father. Even after he assisted me during the labor and delivery, he was the first one to change Hunter's diaper. Danny wanted to stay home with us but he was only given the weekend off. So there I was, alone with Hunter at our little house nestled among fields in our small, rural town. The closest neighbor was a mile away.

Pacing the kitchen floor, I held Hunter and glanced at the phone. Should I call someone? Who should I call? Would it do any good?

The fact that my family couldn't be there bothered me greatly.

Why can't I have them here when I need them?

If only my mom wasn't working full-time at night or my mother-in-law, Kathy, was not recovering from pneumonia. Why did she have to get sick of all times? Why didn't I have aunts close by or my biological grandparents still alive? Not that the last thought mattered. My parents had closed the door on their biological family a long time ago. I couldn't blame them. They were both raised by foster families. These families cared for their basic needs, but not their emotional ones. I'm sure they felt betrayed.

I wondered if this was why I struggled with my emotions. Were my own anger issues born from watching my dad lose his temper? Did I learn these negative behaviors from him? Was that why I reacted so quickly in anger and thought that it was normal? Truthfully, I didn't know any other way.

I wanted to throw Hunter in his crib and leave him there forever, not knowing what else to do. While I didn't throw him in his crib, I did lay him there and walked away. With the incessant crying, I reached a breaking point, and I had no one to turn to for immediate help, except for God, that is. Suddenly I remembered He was always with me, if I acknowledged Him.

"God, please help me! I do not want to be a mom who hurts her child. I want to be a good mom. Show me what to do!"

I wondered if I taking Hunter for a drive would soothe him. The weather was cold, but I could bundle him up and turn on the heat in the car. I had heard other parents say a drive calmed their children.

I grabbed Hunter's sleeper coat and infant car seat from the floor by the kitchen door and hurried back to his room. I picked him up with shaky hands and started putting on his coat.

"Hunter, Mommy is sorry I yelled at you. We are going for a drive. Is that what you need?" Hunter still wailed.

A few moments later, with superhuman strength calming my nerves, I had Hunter snuggled in his car seat. I carried my bundle of screaming joy out to the car and with a quick snap of the car seat into its base, he was secure. Hoping some heat and music surrounding him might comfort him, I eased the car out onto the road. Headlights shining in the winter night, I drove the back roads, not paying attention to the radio or where I was heading. I simply dwelled on what just had happened.

Why did I get so mad at Hunter? He was only a baby. I wanted to be a good mom, but I had already failed him. He didn't know what he was doing or why, nor did I. I wished answers would just be there when I needed them. It occurred to me that maybe they actually were. Hadn't God shown me what to do just now?

I looked back at Hunter who was sleeping soundly. I was relieved for the moment, but what would I do next time? And what would I do when Danny was gone for extended periods of time for training and drills with the Air National Guard? Hunter often fussed for thirty minutes or more.

The first night home, he barely slept. He didn't want his bottle. I rocked him, offered him his pacifier, checked to make sure he was not too warm or too cold, and changed his diaper. A family friend, who had stayed with us that second night, had offered some suggestions, like putting on his little mittens so he wouldn't scratch himself. He slept better after that, but never for more than two or three hours consecutively.

I could barely keep my eyes open. I couldn't think straight and I could see no way of how I was going to survive this parenting thing. The future looked bleak. I felt alone and isolated. Tears rolled down my cheeks. I had to change. I could not allow my actions based on my feelings to cause hurt to another person, especially not to my brand new baby.

We finished our drive and I took my sleeping boy inside. The quiet calm allowed me a moment to study Hunter's adorable little features. He had my long nose and short chin, but his ears were more like Danny's, which stuck out slightly. Light brown fuzz covered his head. Most of our family and friends said he looked like me (petite and brunette) while a few others said he resembled Danny (tall and dark haired). I said he simply looked like Hunter. He was so cute! No one really blamed me for showing him off to anyone that would listen, and for constantly snapping pictures of him. It was easier in the momentary quiet to feel the full truth: I loved him completely. Then I prayed…

"Dear Father,

Thank You for helping me take care of Hunter. I know now more than ever that I cannot raise him without You by my side. I may not yet be the good mom I want to be, but if I rely on You, ask for Your wisdom which brings peace, I know I can change. I want to be more submissive to Your plans and be more considerate of Hunter's needs. I want to be full of mercy and be sincere in my love for him. I want to produce spiritual fruit that is already within me. I really do love him. He is such a blessing and so precious. I don't want to abuse this wonderful gift you have given me. Please help me! In Jesus' name. Amen."

CHAPTER TWO

PROVIDING FOR A GROWING FAMILY

~

"The wicked borrow and do not repay but the righteous give generously..." Psalm 37:21

"And my God will meet all your needs according to his glorious riches in Christ Jesus." Philippians 4:19

"Hey, buddy," I said, feeding Hunter his bottle in the living room. "Sorry Mommy is upset a lot. I'm worried about paying the bills and whether or not Daddy and I will have enough for your diapers, clothes, wipes, bottles, and formula. Formula costs a lot of money. I can't breastfeed because of my medication. I don't want to pass it through to you. I just wish we could catch a break. I want to give you the best."

Tears ran down my face. I quickly wiped them away. Hunter gazed at me with his big, hazel eyes, sucking on his bottle. He didn't understand the conversation but that did not bother me. Admitting my fears out loud served as a comfort, no matter who listened. At least with Hunter I didn't have to answer judgmental questions.

I wonder what everyone else is thinking right now. They're probably laughing and talking about how stupid Danny and I are. Or maybe they're complaining about having to give us money all the time when we both work. They are right. We shouldn't be having money problems.

I propped Hunter on my shoulder and patted his back. He let out a deep burp and fell asleep.

Danny and I had fought to pay off our debt for several months and hoped the situation would improve, believing God would miraculously deliver us from the debt's grasp. Despite prayers and extra funds from the church and our families, the situation appeared hopeless. I knew we couldn't keep running to others to save us, but what else could we do? We needed saving but only God could do that. That is, if He cared enough to do it.

"God, can You please help us here! Do you even care?" I prayed. "I need some hope. I'm about to give up. Why did You give Hunter to us if we couldn't afford to have him? What happened to supplying all our needs according to your glorious riches in Christ Jesus?"

Eventually our Jehovah Jireh did relieve us from the debt, but the deliverance did not happen through the provision of money. It came through what we considered a last resort: bankruptcy. I remember that day, a month before Hunter was born, when Danny and I looked at each other as we sat at the kitchen table, knowing we had no other choice.

"Do we need to file...bankruptcy?" I asked Danny, the word 'bankruptcy' falling awkwardly off my tongue.

"I don't know what else to do." Danny answered, shrugging his shoulders. He lifted his glasses up and rubbed his eyes. "But I heard about a good lawyer we can talk to. He's a Christian. The only thing is that his office is forty-five minutes away. Let us see what he says. Maybe we can get out of it somehow since the credit counseling place didn't help," he replied.

"I can't believe we have to do this! I never thought we were the kind of people to mess up our finances this bad. If only you hadn't used all those credit cards. I know you had them before we married, but still, I was always so careful with my credit card. If I used it, I paid it off every month. Now look where we are." I paused to gather all my hurt and accusatory thoughts before I continued. I had stood up and crossed my arms.

"Maybe you shouldn't have changed jobs a few months ago. Now we have less income. God knows we didn't do this on purpose. Why didn't He come through like He promised in the Bible? What about answering our prayers and meeting our needs? Some God He is!" I blurted out. I dropped my hands down to my sides and clenched them into fists.

"Lisa, don't blame God. We are the ones who used the credit cards."

"I know, but we tried to pay them off and we realized our mistake. Doesn't God see that?"

"Of course. And you never know, this could be a blessing in disguise," Danny said to reassure me. He stood up and came over to my side, grabbing into me a hug. "Other people have filed bankruptcy and ended up better than before. I'm sure we will be okay."

"I hope so. This is no fun. That's for sure. I don't like learning lessons the hard way," I said, relaxing in his arms.

We had waited until after Hunter's birth to speak with the lawyer. I glanced at his office from the parking lot and then cautiously headed in. Danny carried in our newborn son, who slept in his infant carrier seat. I gripped the diaper bag and a folder of paperwork; documentation of bills, income, and other expenses. With each step, I prayed for God to give us wisdom and to use this experience to teach us a new way to better care for Hunter. Once inside, the lawyer invited us into his office and gestured at the chairs.

"Please sit down. How old is your cutie there?" he asked, nodding in Hunter's direction.

"He's one month old," I told him beaming from ear to ear.

"Well, he's quite precious."

"Thank you," I said, handing him the folder.

Let's get this over with. I can't believe I'm here.

The lawyer carefully studied our paperwork before telling us the news. The whole time I kept fidgeting and picking at my fingernails.

"Yeah, you qualify for Chapter 13 Bankruptcy," he finally said.

Oh no. He's confirming my worst fears.

Good news, you will only lose the four wheeler and the new truck."

That's it? We can live without those items. All I care about is keeping the house.

Danny and I both breathed a huge sigh of relief. There was hope after all. But how would I tell our friends and family? Yes, they knew we struggled financially, but no one wants to admit filing bankruptcy. I didn't want to admit I failed. How embarrassing!

As hard as it was to file bankruptcy, God used the experience as an eye opener. We learned to change our spending habits, especially if we wanted financial freedom. No more credit cards and all debt paid off as soon as possible. We needed to give generously as the righteous do and trust God to provide. We didn't want to fall back on our pledge to pay back what we owed or borrow money when God supplied all of our needs already. We wanted to provide adequately for our family and model the Biblical principles of money.

Once we completed the bankruptcy process, the weight lifted off our shoulders. Our financial situation improved from that point on. The Air National Guard hired Danny as a full-time service technician (mechanic). He reported for duty on November 1, 2004. The job paid well, offered good benefits, and provided the job security we needed for our young family.

"Dear Father,

Thank You for reminding me to rely on You for everything, including our finances. I am sorry we accumulated all this debt, and I understand why You didn't rescue us. You are not a fairy godmother. You don't often wave a magic wand and make it all better. Sometimes You use bad circumstances to show us the good way to live. I am thankful You provided us what we needed through the church and our family while we filed bankruptcy. Thank You for teaching us the proper way to handle money. I will do all I can to trust You more and be more generous with my giving. I will not worry about money. In Jesus' name. Amen."

CHAPTER THREE

SURPRISE!

~

"Every good and perfect gift is from above, coming down from the Father of the heavenly lights, who does not change like shifting shadows." James 1:17

With the bankruptcy scare at an end, I thought I could relax. I was wrong. Remember the night I wanted to throw Hunter in his crib and wondered how I'd manage without Danny for any length of time? I found out in September of 2004. He was serving in Montana, fixing a radar tower for the Air National Guard.

Hunter was seven months of age and just learning to sit up. He still woke up at night. Without a doubt, I definitely needed God's help, especially in the days leading up to Danny's departure, and in the first part of his absence.

With dread, I watched Danny pack his belongings the day he left, trying to hold back the tears. My stomach growled and my eyelids drooped. I hadn't eaten or slept the past two days. No matter how much I hid my feelings, Danny could tell I was not happy.

"Are you okay?" Danny asked me, shoving more clothes into his oversized army bag, which rested on the bed.

"I don't know," I said before sobs broke loose and shook my whole body. This was not how I wanted to say goodbye.

"It'll be okay. I'll be back before you know it," he said reassuringly, hugging me tight.

"I...know...but it...seems like forever."

"I'll call you every night, okay?" Danny said, stepping back and looking me in the eyes. He wiped a tear away. I didn't want him to let go.

"Okay. I'll miss you."

"I'll miss you too...love you."

"I love you, too."

I stood by the kitchen window while Danny walked out the door to the car in the driveway. He loaded his bag into the trunk. He folded his six foot, two inch frame into the driver's seat, started the engine, and drove out onto the highway. The car slowly disappeared from sight. I turned to look at Hunter, who was playing in his exercise saucer by the living room window. Tears still pooled in my eyes but I didn't want to cry in front of him. The overwhelming fear and loneliness almost suffocated me. Would I really be all right?

"Well, Bubby, it looks like it's just you and me for two weeks. I love you but I'm so glad there is only one of you to take care of! You're enough for now. We'll be fine," I said to comfort me more than him.

He flashed me a big smile.

Then reality hit me. I would become a single mom whenever Danny had to be away.

Welcome to the world of a military family! Lord, please be with me! Make the next two weeks go by fast.

Those two weeks did go by fast, but they were not without their challenges. Hunter did not sleep well due to teething and an upper respiratory infection that almost turned into pneumonia. Since he didn't sleep well, I didn't sleep well. I also committed what some consider a parental sin. I let Hunter sleep with me. I don't care if it was wrong. I needed at least a little sleep.

My new job at the early childhood learning center was easier by far than the ECSE (Early Childhood Special Education) teaching job I had left on the whole, but these kids tested my patience just as the ones at the other job had. I reminded myself I was doing everything for God, not man, or in this case, child.

As if that wasn't enough stress in my life, the car I usually drove required several repairs. My in-laws willingly offered their cars for us to use but I wanted to slump down in the seat and hide when I drove those cars. They were like driving yachts on the road–yachts named 'Old Person's Huge Car.' They were dependable, however, so I tried not to complain.

At least the need for borrowed cars was only temporary. A minor blessing, but a blessing nonetheless.

I had some real positives during this time though. Besides Danny calling me at night as promised, my family kept me company and helped me on occasion. Some of my new coworkers and I had become friends and they provided adult conversation on a daily basis. The adult interaction was a lifesaver for me, as was Hunter's swing.

It was still a difficult time though as I said before. With Hunter still having long crying episodes I was left feeling inadequate and helpless. "What am I going to do with you?" I asked him, hoping he might give me a hint of what to do. My heart pounded in my chest and my body tensed up. I had to figure out something as soon as possible.

God, I know You are with me. I feel alone and isolated right now but if You can, show me what to do.

"Mommy has to wash dishes, put clothes away, and pay some bills. I can't get this stuff done with you crying. You shouldn't be hungry and you just had a diaper change. You know what? You like the swing. Shall we go swing?" I asked him, not expecting a response other than his continued fussing.

But just moments later, after I strapped him in the swing and turned it on, he quieted down. His eyes slowly closed as he fell asleep.

Thank You, Lord! Peace and quiet at last. I almost lost it with him. Man, I sure wish Danny was here.

As one might guess, saying I missed my soldier was an understatement. Never was I more thrilled to see him than when he returned home from Montana. I loved having him back. We were together again. I didn't have to be afraid or feel lonely. More wonderful though, was that I had a partner to help with Hunter!

A month passed, and I noticed myself beginning to drag through the days at work. I thought the fatigue came from the constant lack of sleep and my frequent trips to the bathroom could be attributed to a possible bladder infection. Both symptoms seemed likely enough. None of this was a big deal and since I had an annual check-up coming soon, I didn't think anymore about it.

"Is there any chance you could be pregnant?" The nurse asked me, guiding me back to the bathroom.

"Oh no. I'm sure of that!" I quickly answered. I mean, yes, I had skipped my birth control because I had no insurance coverage with my new job, but the thought of conceiving didn't seem possible.

After leaving my urine sample, I sat on the exam table, wearing my stylish paper gown and drifting off to la la land.

Today is Pearl Harbor day, and Mom turned 62 yesterday…

"We cannot perform your PAP," my doctor informed me, entering the room.

I raised my eyebrows. "Uh…Why?"

"You are pregnant."

"I'm pregnant?" I asked in shock.

"Your pregnancy results came back positive. Are you okay with this pregnancy?" she asked with concern. I guess my shock showed.

"Oh yes. I'm happy, really. I'm surprised, that's all. I just can't believe I'm pregnant. I've only been off my birth control a month. Of course, now I know why I've been feeling so tired and going to the bathroom more often. Everything makes sense. Hunter is going to be a big brother! Can you tell me how far along I am?"

My OB/GYN examined me, estimating my baby to be about seven week gestation. My due date was July 13th. Hunter and his younger sibling would be about seventeen months apart. The shock was replaced with total excitement that could not be contained. I had to share the news.

"Danny, you will not believe this. I'm pregnant!" I exclaimed to him by phone, as I rushed to the car. (He had stayed home with Hunter.)

"Are you serious?" he almost shouted. He sounded just as surprised as me.

"Yes. The doctor couldn't do the exam. The pregnancy test came back positive."

"How far along are you?"

"About seven weeks. My due date is July 13th."

"That is great. I am happy. Really, I'm happy."

Regardless of the pregnancy being unexpected, Danny and I shared the news with joy in our hearts. Our family, friends, coworkers, and church family congratulated us. We even told our Bible Study group.

While my face glowed with excitement, it wasn't long before my doubts began to arise within me. Could I handle two small children when I struggled to care for one? God must want me to be a mom. He sure has a sense of humor! I believed I would be okay in time, though. In spite of the anger and anxiety issues plaguing my life, eventually I would be the mom I wanted to be. God trusted me, so I had to trust him to do what was best for me.

"Dear Father,

Surprise! I'm pregnant again. And to think I worried about having kids because of my irregular periods. Sorry for doubting You. You have proven yourself again. I do want to ask You to keep this baby healthy and for him to sleep well at night. I don't think I can survive getting up with two babies. I'm already exhausted. Please help me get through these next seven months and the days after the birth. I can't do this alone. Thank You for this good and perfect gift from above. Thank You that You do not change. You are steadfast. I want to be like You. In Jesus' name. Amen."

CHAPTER FOUR

EVERYTHING ALWAYS WORKS OUT

∾

"And we know that in all things God works for the good of those who love him, who have been called according to his purpose." Romans 8:28

"I sought the LORD, and he answered me; he delivered me from all my fears." Psalm 34:4

My high hopes for 2005 being a better year were hard to hold on to. The day before Hunter's birthday party, Danny went to mail bill payments and to stop at the bank for cash. When he didn't return within the hour, I began pacing the kitchen floor and glancing out the window. Hunter napped in his crib.

Where is Danny? He should be here by now. I hope he didn't run into someone he knows and start talking to them.

He needs to come home. We have to get ready for Hunter's party tomorrow.

The ringing of the phone startled me.

It must be Danny.

"Hello?" I answered.

"Is this Lisa Weitkamp?" A strange man's voice asked.

"Yes."

"This is the State Highway Patrol. Your husband Dan has been in an accident. He appears to be okay, but he agreed to ride in the ambulance to the hospital so they could check him out."

"What happened?" I felt my stomach twisting into knots.

"He hit some ice on the road and the car slid off into a culvert pipe."

"You think he's okay?"

"He was walking and talking. I would say he is fine."

"Can you tell me how bad the car is damaged?"

"From what I could tell, it is totaled."

My heart sank. "Thank you, officer."

"You are welcome. Sorry for the news, but be thankful your husband is okay."

"I know. Bye."

Of course, I thanked God that Danny didn't sustain any serious injuries. The car, though, was not so lucky. I couldn't stop myself from dwelling on that loss.

All right God, now what? We just paid the car off last month. I thought this year would be better. Does this mean we have to buy another car and make car payments again? Please guide us through this problem and not let it ruin Hunter's party tomorrow.

Yes, my little Bubba turned one! We celebrated the occasion a week early because Danny had to leave at the beginning of February for a two week mission in Arizona and would be gone on Hunter's actual birthday.

We kept plans for the party as scheduled and several friends and family attended. Hosting a child's birthday party was unchartered territory for me. I tried to put on a happy face for Hunter and the guests. When no one offered to help me pass out the presents, cut the cake, or scoop the ice cream, I began to get resentful and angry. I didn't know how to respond appropriately while they all stood around, ignoring my sour demeanor. I was so preoccupied with putting on my act, it never occurred to me to ask for help, from the people or God.

"You people could help a little here," I mumbled. "And why can't Danny do something? No, he's just standing around like everyone else, watching me run around like a chicken with my head cut off!"

Most of my under-my-breath comments were directed at Danny. Of all people, he should've helped. Then, as I wallowed in my self-pity and placed Hunter's cake on the table, a State Highway Patrol car pulled into the driveway.

What is he doing here on a Sunday? We are getting ready to sing to Hunter and give him his cake. This couldn't wait?

"Hey Danny, there's a police car in the driveway."

"What?"

"Yes. Look," I said, pointing in that direction.

"What the heck?"

Danny put on his coat and strolled out to the car. The patrol man climbed out of his car and began talking to Danny. Everyone at the party observed the scene outside, curious as to what was happening. Hunter sat in his high chair, oblivious to the circumstances. Grandma Weitkamp entertained him with his new toys. The rest of us witnessed the officer grab his notepad and write on it. Danny reluctantly held out his hand, taking the paper from the man in uniform. His face scrunched up in a scowl. He marched back into the house and threw the paper down.

"He gave me a ticket!"

"For what," I asked in astonishment.

"For driving recklessly."

"How could he do that? He wasn't there!"

"I know, I know. But they examined the accident scene and said I drove too fast for the road conditions."

"Can they do that?"

"I guess so. I'm going to fight it, too."

"Well, we need to finish the party. I'm sure everyone needs to leave soon. We can deal with this later."

The guests hadn't said much since Danny returned to the house except to offer their sympathy. In our opinion, he didn't deserve that ticket. The roads were slick from ice and snow.

Anyhow, we continued the celebration of our sweet baby boy. He wasn't sure what to think of the chocolate cake until he tasted a bite. Then he dug in with both hands! His first taste of the rich, sugary goodness. He was so happy!

I, however, was not. I still was fuming about Danny not helping me. He could have helped even if he did just get a ticket.

"Danny! Can you help please?"

"Can't you do this?" he hollered at me.

"I only need you to scoop the ice cream."

"Well, come on Lisa. I just got a ticket. Leave me alone!" He pushed several plates off the counter and stormed off.

Some of our family offered to help then, but as soon as everyone ate the cake and ice cream, they left. What a disaster! Only Hunter enjoyed the party. Even if no one else had a good time, the Birthday Boy had smiled, laughed, and played in his cake. He was too young to understand recent events. While I was happy for him, I decided to host his next party at a different location. Trying to do this at my house proved to be a mistake.

As the saying goes, though, there is silver lining to every cloud. A month later, I received news that I could cash out my 401K from the school being that I was no longer employed with them. While processing the cash out, which required a few weeks, Danny and I asked God to show us what to do about our vehicle situation and how to best use the 401K money. We wanted to save the money but we needed it too much. At the time, we did not have enough faith in God to provide the funds in a different way. Sometimes, even today, I wonder if our lives would have been different if we had waited on Him to carry out his plans instead of relying on our own resources. Who knows?

In the end, everything worked out. We bought a 2000 GMC Jimmy. The SUV was purchased from a local dealer where a fellow church member worked as a salesman. Small world! He found a company that accepted bankruptcy applicants. We signed a finance plan to make payments for five years, not minding the high interest rate added into the payments or the prospect of enduring monthly statements again. Driving our own vehicle was worth the sacrifice. (We had been using our in-law's land yachts again.)

We also bought another new car, a 2005 Chevy Aveo. The small, economically friendly car offered dependability and less frequent trips to the gas pump. Danny traveled almost 180 miles round-trip, to work every day, and we believed owning the car only made sense. We went from one car payment to two car payments! Not what I envisioned for 2005 for sure, but I felt we would be fine. Plus, my 401K money arrived shortly thereafter, and we used it to pay off bills and buy new items for the house.

We purchased a beautiful used bedroom set, a new washer and dryer set, and a breakfast nook for the kitchen. I can still see Hunter "helping" his Daddy assemble the new table.

I loved Hunter more each day, even if his sleepless nights tested my diminishing patience.

By this time, we had found out Hunter would have little brother as well. I would have two little Danny Juniors running around. Oh boy!

"Dear Father,

Thank You for showing us what to do about the 401K money. I like driving my own vehicle. I like the washer and dryer set, the bedroom set, and the breakfast nook too. I am so thankful for Hunter and our new baby boy. I am excited to see him in July, but nervous. Help me transition into having two kids. I still need to get better about asking for help from You or anyone else! I feel bad about the party. Please forgive me for being rude to Danny and our guests. Good thing they're family! I'm sorry for not trusting You to provide. You would think I would have this figured out by now. Help me increase my faith in You for all aspects of my life. In Jesus' name. Amen."

CHAPTER FIVE

DOUBLING DIAPER DUTY

∿

"Take my yoke upon you, and learn from me, for I am
gentle and humble in heart, and you will find rest for
your souls." Matthew 11:29

"To the LORD I cry aloud, and he answers me from his
holy hill. I lie down and sleep; I wake again, because the
LORD sustains me." Psalm 3:4-5

"You're going to have two babies in diapers at once.
Have you thought about toilet training Hunter?" my
mother-in-law, Kathy asked me one day while talking on the
phone with her. "I had Danny and the other two boys trained
when they were one."

*Good for you. I know you mean well, but people don't
train their kids as early as they used to. Times are different
now than when you raised the boys.*

I gritted my teeth. "Hunter is not ready to use the toilet yet. I am perfectly capable of changing diapers on two kids. I do it every day at the learning center," I replied.

She wasn't the only one doubting my mothering abilities. Other family and friends joined in with their opinions. While I knew deep down I could handle the challenge and these other people weren't trying to make me feel bad, I needed encouragement, not negative feedback.

My family and friends forgot I changed up to eight kids' diapers a day in the two-year-old classroom at the center. Changing diapers for two kids would not be a problem for me. Why did these people act as if the world would end because I had to change diapers on more than one child? What did parents do with twins? Or triplets? Or even sextuplets!? Sorry people, Hunter wasn't ready for toilet training.

As my due date with Colt drew closer, Danny traveled to Nebraska and Arizona again for the National Guard, but our family of three still found time to visit Branson. We rode on Thomas the Tank Engine, who stopped in town, and swam at the Lost Valley Lake Resort.

Hunter finally learned to walk at sixteen months, with only one month away from meeting his baby brother. He had been executing the army crawl until thirteen months of age. Then he crawled with his stomach off the floor. He met these milestones later than most of his peers, but he was still within normal limits according to his doctor. He said a few words, too, including his first word of "no." Was that an indication of stubbornness to come?

By the first of July, I was more than ready to see my second baby boy, who did not seem too concerned about meeting the rest of us. While the pregnancy had been free of major problems, being nine months pregnant in the dead heat of summer is *agonizing*.

"Danny, I think I'm in labor. I'm having contractions every five minutes," I said. It was two weeks before my due date.

"Are you sure?" he asked, trying to loosen a blade on the lawn mower. He was lying on the grass out by the driveway. "Get off, you stupid blade! Why can't anything be simple? Just make it simple!" He stood up and brushed his pants off.

"Uh…I don't know if I'm in labor, but I think I am. Remember I was induced with Hunter so I don't know what normal labor feels like."

"Well, let me clean up and we'll go."

"I'll grab the bags."

We left Hunter with our family and hurried to the hospital.

"I think I'm in labor!" I told the Labor and Delivery nurse, my face flushed with excitement.

"All right, let us check you out. When did the contractions start?" she asked, showing me a room to use.

"About three this afternoon."

"How far apart are they?"

"Five minutes." I lay down on the bed. Danny claimed the recliner by the bed, expecting to stay awhile.

The nurse continued to update my information while checking my vitals. I gave her a urine sample. A few minutes later she returned.

"You're dehydrated," she told me. "You're not in labor."

"I'm not?" My face lost its color.

I'm not in labor? This can't be true. I don't feel dehydrated.

"No. Dehydration can cause false labor."

I looked at Danny. He stared at the floor, frowning.

"Sorry dear."

"No. That's okay," he said, looking up and smiling. "As long as you and the baby are fine, that's all that matters. He'll come when he's ready."

"Well, I hope he'll be ready soon."

A week later, I had a second false alarm stemming from a bladder infection. A few days after my second false alarm, coincidentally on my due date, my OB/GYN examined me for my 40th week checkup.

Lord, please have the doctor induce me. I want to get this over with.

After the doctor finished her exam, I heaved myself up, bulging belly and all, and dressed myself. The doctor left the room briefly. As I waited for her to come back, I nervously fidgeted with my shirt. When she re-entered the room, I searched her eyes, wanting to find the answer before she spoke. She smiled. That was a positive sign.

"Everything looks good. I guess you are ready to have this baby?"

"Definitely!" I agreed.

"We can induce you, just not tonight. The rooms are full. We can schedule you for tomorrow at midnight. Is that all right?"

What choice did I have? Colt was not coming by his own will apparently. "Sure," I spoke quietly, trying to hide my disappointment.

The next twenty-four hours could not have ended fast enough, especially when I started feeling sick the next morning (which I later realized came from the onset of labor). Danny stayed home from work to care for Hunter, and I had already begun my maternity leave earlier that week. I lounged around the entire day like a lazy bum, but all I cared about was surviving another labor and delivery.

Lord, please help the labor and delivery go well. I want both of us to be healthy and for there to be no complications.

The time arrived. At midnight on the night of July 14th, 2005, the nurse induced me with Pitocin. I spent only three hours in active labor (the epidural did not work so three hours was long enough!). At 4:25 a.m., July 15th, Coltin Nathaniel, shortened to Colt, entered the world weighing 8 pounds, 7 ounces, and measuring 22 inches long. A big boy! He had a head full of dark hair and the chubbiest cheeks. He quickly earned one of his nicknames, Chunka Bunk. He was bigger than his brother, who had only weighed 8 pounds 1 ounce, and measured 21 inches at birth. Unlike his brother, he wanted to eat right after he came out. His appetite would be of no concern to me.

Colt proved to be an easy baby, overall, and I appreciated every moment with him. I loved him more each day, even with his health issues.

"Are you ready to burp Coltie?" I sat him up on my lap while gently holding his head under his chin. I patted his back. He let out a big belch followed by a large volume of formula, which he projectile vomited onto the carpet.

"Oh no, not again. Are you okay, Buddy?" I placed him in a beanie bag chair and snatched up a kitchen towel. I soaked it with water and wiped off the floor the best I could. "Should Mommy take you to the doctor? You know what, let me call him and set up an appointment."

The next day's appointment proved to be frustrating. "He's gaining weight so I don't see the need to prescribe him medication or change his diet," his pediatrician said.

That's easy for you to say! You're not the one cleaning up the messes! Why can't he just take something to stop this? It can't be healthy. And you're not the one with a baby who throws up half his bottle in the middle of restaurants, all over the floor while other customers stare. You're not the one whose husband has to change his shirt because his son threw up all over him again.

I had to accept the fact there was nothing I could do about Colt spitting up. However, despite his digestive issues, Colt remained calm. What a difference there was between him and

Hunter, and not just the size. Yes, Hunter looked like a giant next to his baby brother, but Colt ate well, slept soundly, and acted more content than Hunter ever did as a newborn. I had to pinch myself to see if I was dreaming. Hunter still woke up during the night while Colt slept through the night at two months old. God had definitely answered my prayer when I asked for Colt to sleep well.

Against others' doubts, and my own fears, caring for two kids proved to be easier than I anticipated. During my maternity leave, when I dropped Hunter off at the center. I caught up on sleep and housework. Through God's prompting, I also created a list of the features I wanted in our next house, which included at least four bedrooms, two bathrooms, a fireplace, and brick exterior.

Danny and I toured several houses and even found one of interest, but the plans fell through. I know why. God wanted us to pray for the right house that we would buy in the future, not at that particular time. Our pastor prayed for us and our future house as well.

We could not have paid for a new house anyhow, because I hadn't received my short-term disability. Danny and I were pinching pennies as the saying goes.

When it came for me to be released back to work, I didn't want to go. Although I liked the job, I wanted be a Stay-at-Home Mom. Would that ever happen? Would God make a way? Was it His will?

"All right boys, Mommy has to go back to work today." I helped Hunter navigate the steps on the deck with one hand and with the other hand, carried Colt in his carrier seat. "I wish I could stay home with you, but we need the money. Maybe someday I can keep you home. At least I can see you since you get to come with me. Isn't that awesome?" I said, trying to sound cheerful. I didn't feel cheerful though. Instead, I felt dread.

Could I do this? Could I keep up with work and taking care of two little ones without going crazy? The Paxil couldn't do miracles.

My first day back went well, yet my heart's desire was to be home. I enjoyed teaching the two-year-olds and chatting with my coworkers, but I sensed my employment there would be coming to an end. I didn't know when or how. I only knew that teaching was no longer my calling or my purpose.

"Dear Father,

Thank You for Colt! He is here and he is healthy! Thank You that he sleeps soundly and has a good appetite. I am concerned about him spitting up though. Would You heal him of that? Or at least show me what to do? I guess I can't have everything perfect. You have to remind me I can't do this parenting thing alone, don't You? I may be growing more as a mom, gaining more confidence, but I still need You! I will still face challenges where I have to rely on Your guidance.

Hunter and Colt are so young yet. I have a long road ahead. Help me enjoy them and love them. Forgive me for getting upset with people who are simply trying to help. Please show us how to fix our finances so I can stay home too. In Jesus' name. Amen."

CHAPTER SIX

MY SICK BOYS

"This was to fulfill what was spoken through the prophet Isaiah: 'He Himself took our infirmities and bore our sicknesses.'" Matthew 8:17

"He said, 'If you listen carefully to the voice of the LORD your God and do what is right in his eyes, if you pay attention to his commands and keep all his decrees, I will not bring on you any of the diseases I brought on the Egyptians, for I am the LORD, who heals you.'" Exodus 15:26

While we waited for the 401K to pay out that spring of 2005, Danny served our country in Arizona and Hunter became sick again with ear infections for what seemed like the millionth time.

"Ugh. Bubba, what am I going to do with you? Your poor ears are not healing. The doctor said you would need tubes if the infection didn't clear up with the medicine. I know you're miserable and so am I! We need to go back to the ENT (Ear, Nose, and Throat doctor)."

"Ba ba ba ba ba," he replied back. He didn't say much other than babbling. With his ears full of drainage he couldn't hear well enough to pick up words, except for that lovely "no."

At the ENT's office, I discussed my concerns with the specialist. "I'm worried about his speech and language skills being delayed. Could he lose his hearing if we don't put tubes in?"

"He could. I think he needs surgery, if you feel comfortable with that."

"Uh, yeah. I wanted you to say that, actually. I think it's the best alternative for him."

"What is a good day for you?" he asked.

"Can we do it after Danny gets back from Arizona? He gets back the end of February."

"Sure. How about March first?"

Just like that, surgery was set.

My "Little Sugars" underwent the surgery with ease. He hardly fussed. The nurses gave him the Best Patient Award. With the tubes in, I waited anxiously to see what improvements we would see. Would Hunter begin to talk more and catch up to his peers? More importantly, would he sleep through the night again? He had just begun to sleep for six to seven hours straight before the ear infections reared their ugly head.

49

"I really hope these tubes do the trick. Wouldn't it be great if Hunter slept all night again?" I said to Danny at dinner one night. I handed Hunter bite-sized pieces of chicken, which he gobbled down. Nothing wrong with his appetite.

"Yes it would. I hope so too," he said as he drank his tea.

At first the tubes worked like a charm. Then, just one month after the surgery, Hunter's ears became infected again.

I called out to God. "Will Hunter's ear infections ever stop? Why is this happening?! Aren't these tubes supposed to stop ear infections? Why is Hunter still experiencing problems? Do You not want him to get better?"

Still, I knew God wanted to heal Hunter. I sought prayer from our pastor and the infection cleared up temporarily. The doctor suspected the condition was caused from sinus and allergy drainage and prescribed Claritin for Hunter.

Hunter developed a few more ear infections in the months to follow, including the months after Colt was born, but I continued believing one day he would experience total healing. I wouldn't give up.

Both boys remained healthy overall, until Thanksgiving, when they both became sick.

Here we go again.

Only this time I had two sick children under my wing instead of one. Hunter was first, requiring a trip to the ER for croup. The ER physician prescribed steroids and breathing treatments for him. I paced for hours holding Hunter as he coughed so hard he could barely catch his breath. Once he recovered from his illness, I let my guard down and felt we had turned a corner.

Whew! I can finally relax!

A week later, Colt developed similar symptoms, only worse. He had bronchiolitis. The doctor prescribed steroids to be used with a nebulizer machine, with the hopes that the breathing treatments would rid the virus from Colt's lungs.

Two days later, Danny and I heard the wheezing sounds increase *after* a breathing treatment. We called the doctor who advised us to take Colt to the emergency room as soon as possible. We dropped Hunter off with Danny's family, and Danny drove us as fast as he legally could to the hospital.

I watched Colt's chest laboring to rise and fall while attempting to hide my fears for his sake. Danny's jaw was tense as he fixed his gaze on the road. We both knew we couldn't let panic take over and we had to stay focused in order to help Colt, who struggled to breathe. I tried not to think of losing him. He was only four months old.

At the emergency room, the doctor told us, "Colt needs to be transferred to Cardinal Glennon. We cannot provide the care he needs here. We'll let you go with him in the ambulance," he said indicating me, "and you can follow," he nodded at Danny.

"Will he be okay?" I pleaded for reassurance.

"He should be fine, ma'am. Cardinal Glennon has the best doctors and equipment available for cases such as your son's."

"Thank you," I said, trying to believe him, though not quite succeeding.

The ambulance ride seemed to drag on for hours though it lasted a mere thirty minutes. I watched my baby boy suck air in, attempting to catch a deep breath. His tiny body looked so small on the adult-sized gurney surrounded by various types of medical equipment. I silently cried out to God, "Please help Colt survive this illness! Open his lungs and bring him back to complete health!"

During the transport, I cringed as the nurse commented to an intern, "See his chest caving in?" She discussed the matter as if it was not a major emergency. Yes, interns gained knowledge from observing, but show some compassion. I wanted to command her to stop talking about my son that way. He was not a research project! Sure, the lights were not flashing or the sirens wailing as the ambulance rolled down the highway so Colt probably was not in immediate danger, but his condition was extremely serious to me, and I wanted them to feel that way too.

It was early morning the next day when we arrived at Cardinal Glennon. I was mentally, emotionally, and physically exhausted. Through blurry eyes, I saw the special crib in Colt's room and people hustling about in the hall. The smell of disinfectant permeated the air.

The staff at the hospital finally explained clearly to us why Colt needed to be admitted and monitored there. They wanted to help us, his parents, to cope with the demands of nursing a critically ill child. The nurses administered the breathing treatments every three or four hours around the clock until

Colt lungs strengthened enough to clear the virus. Sometimes Colt spit up mucus so we coordinated his feedings to be after those times. It was exhausting round the clock work, but the wheezing episodes subsided.

Within two days of undergoing these intense treatments Colt was discharged to go home. He was okay.

"Lord, thank You for using the doctors and nurses to heal my son," I prayed.

By the time I could work again, I had used all my sick time. I had to take off two days without pay. As anyone knows, one of the worst times to lose income is at Christmas. I wondered if we would have the funds to buy presents. But, then again, *why* did I worry? Hadn't He always met our needs?

As He promises in Scripture, God provided enough money for us to purchase plenty of presents! I treasure many good memories of family opening presents and all of us eating delicious holiday treats on Colt's first Christmas. What more could I desire besides another year of being a mom to my two spunky little boys? Nothing. Nothing at all.

When Danny's mom called to check on us, I answered honestly, "We are fine. Really we are okay. Thank you for checking on us."

As 2006 began, Colt and Hunter grew daily. Hunter ran around constantly. Colt started to crawl, trying to keep up with his big brother. He spoke his first word, "Da-Da."

My Chunka Bunk developed normally in spite of his digestive issues, ear infections, and wheezing episodes. He still had quite the adorable chubby cheeks! As for Hunter, his tubes had completely fallen out (as they were supposed to) but his ear infections had returned.

Danny and I scheduled an appointment with the ENT for Hunter and another appointment with the pulmonologist for Colt.

The pulmonologist diagnosed Colt with Post Viral Wheezing, which meant anytime he contracted a virus, he would wheeze and require breathing treatments and/or an inhaler. Both boys underwent surgery at the end of March to have tubes placed in their ears. They handled their surgeries well, and I prayed for the tubes to work this time.

Hunter's ears eventually healed but then his sinuses became infected. So much for him sleeping all night! His poor little nose ran constantly with nasty drainage and the doctor had to prescribe antibiotics again. As before, the medicine didn't complete kill the virus and unfortunately he was sick again.

Danny and I met with the ENT and picked a day for Hunter's adenoidectomy. Despite being around his brother who became sick with bronchitis, Hunter remained healthy for the procedure, which happened that summer. Except for the anesthesia not wearing off until that evening, he recovered without any problems. The ENT specialist told us Hunter's adenoids were significantly enlarged and that removing them was a smart decision. The tonsils were left behind. Although they were infected, the ENT wanted to wait.

Doctor, you better be right. I do not want any more fevers, sleepless nights, unplanned trips to the family doctor, or dose after dose of antibiotics. I am way past being done with this headache.

Hunter's health appeared to be on the mend. The steps were small, but the Ultimate Healer used this experience to gradually increase my faith in the area of health. Although He still hadn't tested me as to what I would do if I Danny or I became sick, this lesson on the boys' well-being taught me that I could not take anything for granted or forget to completely trust Him in all aspects of my life.

"Dear Father,

Thank You, thank You, thank You for saving my boys! Thank You for Danny's support and for the support of his family. I was so scared! Just when I thought everything was going well, the boys became seriously sick. I confess my doubts about them getting better and my lack of trust that You would heal them. I should've been praying for their health all along. Maybe this wouldn't have happened. I need to pray for protection and health. I need to pray all the time, not just when there's a problem, but before there's a problem. You are the Ultimate Healer and I have to trust You to keep the boys well. You don't want them to be sick and neither do I. Please keep us all healthy. In Jesus' name. Amen."

CHAPTER SEVEN

MOMMY AND DADDY ARE SICK

❧

"O LORD my God, I called to you for help and you healed me." Psalm 30:2

"Be merciful to me, LORD, for I am faint; O LORD, heal me, for my bones are in agony." Psalm 6:2

*D*anny *had left work not feeling well and was back at home for the day. I was at the pharmacy for yet another prescription for Hunter when Danny called.*

"Mike is taking me to the hospital. I really can't take the pain anymore. My stomach hurts and it's really painful on my right side."

"The hospital? I thought you were having heartburn or just had a stomach virus," I said. "For you to go to the hospital it must be serious."

I thought guiltily back to earlier that day.

Man, I shouldn't have accused him of being a big baby. I showed him no sympathy. Now he's going to the hospital with who knows what. Appendix? Hernia? Lord, please take care of Danny for me!

I arranged for my mom to watch the boys before hurrying to be by Danny's side. Mike, his older brother, stood in the hall outside his room. Mike looked like their mom Kathy, who was slightly taller than me, with short dark hair, glasses, and a round face.

"How is he?" I asked Mike.

"They've already done blood tests and a CT Scan. He has appendicitis and it's not good. They've set up surgery to remove it tonight because it's on the verge of bursting."

I tiptoed into the room. Danny rested on the bed. I stood by his side, right where I wanted to be.

"How are you doing, dear?" I held his hand.

He opened his eyes. "I'm fine. How are you?" he said weakly.

"Nervous. I feel so bad that I didn't believe you were really that sick. I love you so much. Will you forgive me?" I begged him.

"It's okay. You didn't know. I'll be fine…I love you too."

Another family member graciously offered to keep Hunter and Colt overnight so I could stay with Danny. I barely slept, praying late into the night for the surgery to be a success, and it was. Praise God for answering my prayer. I knew He had protected Danny from harm. What a relief!

While my husband's life was no longer in danger, he still had to spend time recuperating from the surgery. I realized the responsibility of maintaining the household and caring for the boys would be totally mine again. No relaxing for me.

Oh Lord, can I handle this? Is it wrong for me to feel like this? Shouldn't I be grateful Danny is here? I could've lost him.

However I might've felt, God gave me what I needed to survive, and Danny soon healed. Everyone was well!

Except for me. That fall, my family doctor referred me to an urologist to deal with the recurring bladder infections.

"With all these bladder infections, I'd say you have a kidney stone. Have you ever had one before?" he asked me in his office that day.

"No. Would this explain my back pain? It started when I was pregnant with Colt. I thought it was from him."

"Yes. Kidney stones can cause dull pain or aches in the back about midway up either side, depending on which kidney."

"What causes kidney stones?" I certainly didn't want to endure this pain if I didn't have to in the future.

"They are usually made up of calcium oxalate. Tea and certain foods, such as broccoli contain it. We will ask you to collect the stones so we can analyze them to be sure. Then we can come up with a plan of action."

"That's fine," I agreed. "So these stones were not from my prenatal vitamins?"

"I don't think so."

"Why am I just now getting them? I didn't have a problem before I became pregnant."

"Probably coincidence. I mean, there's a chance the pregnancy might've magnified the situation but it's not the cause. We will schedule an X-ray where you'll be injected with a contrast, or dye you might say. It will highlight any abnormalities."

As I lay on the table, waiting for the technicians to inject the contrast into my arm, I quietly sent a request to God. *Lord, please help them find answers as to what is causing my bladder infections. May they know what to do and know how to treat the condition.*

The technicians snapped a few slides, each time talking intently but quietly amongst each other.

Hmmm, what they are saying? Oh well, I'm sure it's nothing.

A nurse called the next day. I had only been home a few minutes and was sorting through the mail when the phone rang. Hunter and Colt had taken off to play in the back of the house.

I answered, recognizing the doctor's number on the caller I.D. I still held a piece of mail in my hand, and I could hear the boys bouncing around in the playroom. They jabbered to each other in their own language.

"We received your X-ray results. We are amazed that you are not doubled over in pain right now. You have a total of *eight* kidney stones. Unfortunately they are too big for you to pass on your own. Five of them are stuck in your right ureter, two more were found in your right kidney, and the last one was found in your left kidney."

"Are you serious!? What does this mean for me? Will I have to have surgery?" I asked in disbelief. I dropped the envelope on the kitchen table and sat down.

"Yes. We have scheduled the procedure to remove the five stones in your right ureter first. Then we will perform the lithotripsy on you to break up the stones within your kidneys. The process to remove these stones requires time, which I am sure you are already short of with the holidays coming up. We recommend the first procedure to be done before Thanksgiving. The good news is the procedure is outpatient and you should be fine to participate in Thanksgiving with your family. The second procedure, the lithotripsy, will be scheduled after Christmas. The main concern at this point is to remove the stones stuck in your ureter. They are causing your bladder infections."

"That explains so much. Thank you." I hung up the phone.

I can't believe this! What am I going to do with so much going on? Who's going to help me? Danny is busy with work. What about the kids and the house?

I called Danny at work.

"You will not believe this! I have eight kidney stones! Five of them are stuck in my right ureter, two more are in my right kidney and one more is in my left kidney. The nurse was amazed I was still standing. I should be doubled over in pain."

"Really? What are they going to do? Can you pass them?"

"Nope. They are too big. I will need three surgeries to remove them. The first one, which will be scheduled before Thanksgiving, will be to remove the five stones in my ureter. The other two will be done after the holidays."

"Boy, you are tougher than me. We'll get through this though. Everything will be okay. I will help you as much as I can. It's my turn to take care of you. You know that right?"

"Yeah, I know. I love you too."

Will he actually take care of me? I'm not used to that. I'm the one always taking care of everyone else. No wonder this happened. I neglected my own health.

As promised, Danny catered to my needs the best he could after the surgery. He didn't always know what the boys needed and I had to show him, but I rested when I could. The doctor successfully freed me of the five traveling kidney stones before Thanksgiving, just in time for me to celebrate with my loved ones.

My heart swelled with joy to gather around the table with all of them. I was not alone. Blessings too many to count or express in words abounded out from the Father's love for me. They were always there even if I didn't always see them. Health, family and love all gave me reasons enough to enjoy life.

"Dear Father,

I know, I know. I have to take care of myself too. I was so busy tending to my family's health problems that I neglected my own well-being. This news reminded me that I am human too. I appreciate Danny and the rest of the family for helping me to recover. I also need to believe Danny when he says he's in pain. I'm sorry for not showing more compassion. Thank You for healing him too.

With most of the kidney stones gone now, I have learned to believe You for my healing and not just for others. That is hard. But I have to be healthy so I can carry out Your work in being a good mom to the boys. I'm not being selfish to pray for my own health. I need You for this area of my life as well. I will quit being self-sufficient and become totally dependent on You. In Jesus' name. Amen."

CHAPTER EIGHT

FUN AND CELEBRATIONS

"This is the day that the LORD has made; let us rejoice and be glad in it." Psalm 118:24

"So I commend the enjoyment of life, because nothing is better for a man under the sun than to eat and drink and be glad. Then joy will accompany him in his work all the days of the life God has given him under the sun." Ecclesiastes 8:15

"Happy New Year again! This year I'm going to believe for wisdom, patience, faith, hope, and love. I want to love my kids, be patient with them and with others, hope for the best, use wisdom with finances, and put complete trust and faith in God. I want to see good finances, my job get better, and for me to CHILL OUT!

Have fun!" I wrote in my journal at the beginning of 2006.

T hough I found time for fun that year, I struggled to enjoy them. Once more, I found my expectations got in the way of the good things which were happening.

It began after Danny's surgery, during the week leading up to Mother's Day. The morning of that special day, I had grumbled to myself, *Why can't I get a day for myself? Why does every other mom get to relax?*

I began lashing out at Danny, even though he wasn't to blame.

"It'd be nice if you could at least do a little something," I complained at Danny. I grabbed my jeans out of the laundry basket and shoved them into the dresser drawer. Hunter and Colt watched TV in the living room.

"Lisa, I just had surgery! Life does not revolve around you. I guess I have to do everything for you. You're not my mom. Why should I do anything for you? That's the kids' job," he argued back.

"They are only two years old and ten months old! What are they going to do? I bet you get to relax on Father's Day. How come you get time to relax and I don't? Not even on special days."

"You can relax anytime you want. You choose not to." He turned his back to me.

"Oh okay. So Hunter and Colt are supposed to fend for themselves? I'm not supposed to go into work? You just don't get it." I slammed the laundry basket onto the floor.

"Yes, I do. You're the one who needs to get some help. Maybe you need to see a psychiatrist."

"I'm not crazy!! I just need a break. I'm tired." Tears welled up in my eyes.

"Well, lay down then. And let me know when you need a break and I'll let you have one."

"Yeah, right. How is that going to happen when you are sick or gone all the time?"

"Will you stop it?" he demanded.

"Fine! Don't expect me to be at your beck and call then!" I marched out of the room to check on Hunter and Colt. They had dumped a whole bucket of Legos on the floor. I wanted to disappear and never come back. A vacation on the beach sounded so tempting then. I could read and visit all the lighthouses.

Though obviously stressed about the lack of rest and relaxation, Danny and I made time to visit with our moms. We enjoyed seeing them. My mom gave me the first season of Little House on the Prairie DVD set and a stain-glass cross with a lighthouse pictured on it. It says "HOPE" in the middle. I hung it on the wall in the bathroom where it reminds me my hope is in God. My brother Paul called and sent me a card, too.

Even though Danny could not bring me breakfast in bed or wake up with Hunter and Colt so I could sleep in for the day, in the end, my Mother's Day that year turned out better than expected. I had my two precious boys and my husband by my side. I couldn't be happier, as long as I redirected my attention on my blessings.

A month later, my side of the family celebrated at Outback Steakhouse for my parents' 35th wedding anniversary (June 27th). Alan, my other brother, planned the party and paid for it too. He sweet talked one of the waitresses into baking a cake, decorating the booth, and placing real flowers on the table. The whole family attended except for Paul, who chose to work instead.

"Is Paul coming?" I asked my mom, who sat across the table from me.

"No. He is working," she answered.

"What do you mean he is working? He couldn't get off for this? I wanted the whole family to be together, something we hardly do anymore. With Dad's health not being the greatest, we never know when he will be gone," I whispered, looking over at my dad to see if he heard. His attention was directed elsewhere, on the boys as they played with their toys. I saw my dad's cane leaning on the table. He was mostly bald with white fuzz on the sides, and he wore glasses. I thanked God I looked more like my mom, who is petite like me, with short black hair and brown eyes. While she wears glasses too, and I don't, at least I wasn't bald!

But anyway, being partially deaf, my dad had missed the conversation between my mom and me. I was safe.

"I know Lis. But I can't make him go. It's his decision."

"He's going to regret it. That's all I got to say."

I put Paul out of my mind and focused on taking pictures from which my mom used to create a large-sized collage. I can still see everyone as they were that day smiling, laughing, and being together. That day will always be treasured.

Less than a month later, I prepared for my sister Lareesa's visit. I'd last said goodbye to her on a cold day in January. Danny, Alan, and I helped her pack that weekend. The only solace from my tears came from knowing I would see her in July.

"Lareesa! Hey sis!" I exclaimed, running to give her a big hug in the airport baggage claim area. She is about six inches taller than me with freckles and brown hair, which she wears about shoulder length.

"I am so happy to see you! Perfect timing with Colt's birthday too. You won't miss his first birthday."

"I know. What can I say? I'm that good." She raised her arm in a victory salute.

"Colt's party is ready to go. Lots of people are coming. I hope you will help me. I don't want a repeat of Hunter's first birthday fiasco."

"Of course. That's what I'm here for."

Danny barbecued for Colt's birthday, while family and friends got reacquainted with each other, sitting in lawn chairs by a big tree in our back yard. They all seemed to forget the reason for the party. Some did not even watch Colt open presents, nor did they sing "Happy Birthday" to him as he blew out his candle and gobbled up his cake. Did they not see him standing in plain view on the deck?

I slipped inside, slamming the door behind me.

Gee, people. You are supposed to be here to celebrate Colt's birthday! Now you ignore him. How rude! I will do the party without you then!

I pushed the negative feelings aside, however. Truly Colt did not care who paid attention to him or who ignored him. He was happy to play with his new toys and eat chocolate for the first time. Lareesa took pictures of his special day and helped me with the party.

Danny, believe it or not, got a ticket for speeding that day.

Is this going to become a family tradition of getting tickets on our children's first birthdays? Then again, Colt is our last child so it doesn't matter.

I still glowered at Danny for costing us another $130 while inwardly I sighed in relief because the police officer did not come to the house this time.

Colt's first birthday proved to be more successful than Hunter's first had been. In fact, Hunter's second birthday had been hassle free because I held it at a local Mexican restaurant, Dos Primos. I was gradually learning how to plan and host a birthday celebration.

To keep the tradition of eating at Mexican restaurants for the boys' birthdays that year, the family, including Lareesa, ate at El Jimador the day after Colt's birthday. We told our waiter about Colt turning one and he brought out a big sombrero for Colt to wear. The other waiters sang to the Birthday Boy. He grinned and laughed at the spectacle. What a nice surprise for my toddler son!

Colt was no longer a baby. He was growing and changing daily. For his one year checkup, he barely whimpered from the shots. His height and weight reached into the upper percentiles. What a big boy! And close to walking too. He started walking alone at thirteen months of age, sooner than his big brother.

From that point on, I had two toddlers to chase!

Meanwhile, Danny and I celebrated our sixth wedding anniversary. My loving husband bought me six flowers, one for each year of marriage, and we shared a lunch of sandwiches and fries at a nearby diner.

"This is so nice. We can eat without some little person crying or dropping his food on the floor." I told Danny.

"Yes. I'm having a good time with you." He leaned over the table and gave me a quick kiss.

We finished celebrating our anniversary that following weekend at Six Flags. Casting Crowns was in concert there so before the show, we braved the roller coaster rides and cooled off at Hurricane Harbor. What a fun day! I cherished all of it. I appreciated our family for keeping the boys as well. The little rascals stayed busy playing with their cousin.

As for my birthday that year, it was the first one in two years that did not leave me feeling discouraged and overwhelmed. My kids were healthy and I didn't have the flu. No supervisor pressured me to "do my job." Danny and I dined at a small Italian restaurant called Stefanina's. We watched The Holiday at the cinema. Danny gave me a dozen red roses and a gift certificate for a thirty minute massage and I sure needed that! Hunter's preschool class designed a big birthday card with the students' signatures, and several people called me to offer birthday wishes. I received much attention.

Not only had I enjoyed my special day, I had enjoyed all the fun and celebrations that year, at least to a certain extent. I still had to let go of my expectations but I was getting there.

"Dear Father,

Thank You for the fun and the celebrations! I enjoyed spending time with my family, including Lareesa. I'm thankful for my parents being together for thirty-five years and for six years of marriage with Danny. We are so blessed with our two boys, who are growing up strong and healthy. Please help me let go of my expectations for special days and not let other's actions determine how I feel. I want to cherish these moments with my loved ones without being upset all the time. Forgive me for looking to them for my happiness. You are my source of joy. Help me remember that. In Jesus' name. Amen."

CHAPTER NINE

GOD WATCHES OUT FOR MY FAMILY

"The thief comes only to steal and kill and destroy; I have come that they may have life, and have it to the full." John 10:10

"For he will command his angels concerning you to guard you in all your ways..." Psalm 91:11

"Danny, where is Colt?" I asked with alarm in my voice, my eyes quickly scanning the yard.

"What do you mean? Isn't he inside with you?"

"No, he came outside a few minutes ago."

"Oh no! Let's check all the buildings. Maybe he wandered off into one of them." Danny dropped his tongs and ran toward the barn. The steaks were left on the grill.

"Colt! Colt!" We both called.

Oh Lord, where is our son? Did someone take him?

We frantically searched every inch of the yard and the house. No Colt. Then an unfamiliar truck pulled into the driveway and a young couple climbed out of the truck with our wayward son.

"We saw this little guy on the side of the road and figured he belonged to you," the lady said.

I swept Colt up in my arms, hugging him close. "Yes! He does! Oh, my gosh. I cannot thank you enough for bringing him back to us! We were scared when we couldn't find him. My husband was barbecuing and didn't know Colt was outside. He thought Colt was inside with me when he had actually followed the dog onto the road.

"You're welcome, and hey, don't feel bad. We have a son about his age and we know how fast they can disappear. We are glad we found him when we did, though. Right after we picked him up, an older couple sped by us in their car. He is one lucky little guy."

So much could have, but didn't happen! I wanted to say Colt was blessed, not lucky. We, as in Danny and I, were blessed as parents, especially during moments such as these where we knew without a doubt God protected our family and kept us all safe from harm.

Colt lived to celebrate his second birthday and his party was a huge success! Twenty-six people attended the event— our family, some coworkers and their families, and friends. Colt happily feasted on his puppy dog shaped cake and tore open his presents. The hit of the day in the present department was the inflatable swimming pool.

The kids splashed and swam in the pool all afternoon. What a perfect day! My gratitude toward everyone could not be expressed enough that day, particularly to my Father. Silently I told Him, "Thank You Lord for watching out for Colt when I failed to do so."

The dog that Colt had followed onto the road was named Destiny and she had belonged to my parents. She was a black, long haired, medium-sized mutt, who was always asking for trouble and frequently found it. Danny and I had agreed to keep her only because my mom and dad moved out of their home of twenty-three years.

The house was slowly falling apart and the landlord did not want to fix it up. My parents settled into a small, one bedroom apartment within the same building as Paul. They were free from the demands of living in a house, such as mowing and cleaning a larger space. I knew they were in a more suitable place, but saying goodbye to their home that held so many memories was difficult. Walking into the empty house broke my heart. My parents would miss everything there, including their dog Destiny. The apartment manager only allowed small dogs.

While I usually adore those cute and furry four-legged creatures called dogs, Destiny was more of a nuisance. She constantly wandered onto the highway where cars sped by at 80 mph. My mom believed she was searching for her owners.

Unfortunately, her fate proved to be as sad as it was predictable. I left for work one morning to discover Destiny's body lying motionless in the grass.

Oh no. How am I going to tell Mom?

As soon as I had a few moments to share the awful news, I slowly dialed my mom's number.

"Hello," she answered cheerfully.

"Mom? I have some bad news for you," I said. I twisted the cap of the pen I held in my hand. I had been planning lessons for the two-year-olds while they napped on their cots.

"What's the matter, Lisa," reading my tone, her tone quickly changed to one of concern.

"Destiny was hit by a car this morning."

"Oh no! Is she okay?"

"No. She didn't make it. I think she died right away from what I can tell. She didn't suffer. I'm so sorry Mom...."

"Oh Lisa, I know it's not your fault. I am sorry it happened too. Destiny was a good dog. I'll sure miss her."

"I know you will. Danny will bury her body in a special place tonight." I hoped that offer would bring comfort to my mom.

"Thank you. I appreciate it."

That night, as promised, Danny buried Destiny in a special place close to the house. No one else appeared to be bothered by the sad turn of events. I, on the other hand, couldn't sleep. I lay in bed, staring at the bedroom ceiling.

Man, I feel awful! Should I have chained her up or let her in the house? Is it my fault? I mean, yes, Destiny liked to stray off into the road. Mom even admitted that. But is it better she is gone? Colt almost got killed because of her. Well, I won't have to worry about that danger anymore. Maybe it's for the best.

As anyone knows, roads can be dangerous and the last place I wanted any of my family to be was stranded on one in the middle of nowhere or their lives taken by reckless drivers. I had a looming fear of my vehicle breaking down while traveling alone, or worse yet, while I had Hunter and Colt with me.

One particular night, I pulled out of the parking lot of the closest Wal-Mart Supercenter from our house, located thirty minutes away in my hometown (a perk of living in the country). The Jimmy started losing power. I had no idea what was wrong. I left the vehicle maintenance up to Danny since he was a mechanic.

My fingers gripped the steering and I checked the gauges every few seconds.

Come on. You can do it. Almost there. Just get me to Mom and Dad's apartment. It's not much further. Five more minutes.

I edged the small truck into the parking spot, and the engine totally died.

Oh great. Now what?

I jumped out and ran to my parent's door. I knocked firmly so they could hear me.

Lord, please let them be home!

My mom came to the door.

"Oh, hi Lis." She sounded startled to see me. "Come in."

I explained, "Something is wrong with the Jimmy. I barely made it here. The engine died and I can't call Danny because he's gone doing some training."

"Let me call Paul," she said, picking up the phone and dialing his number. When Paul answered, she explained what I told her.

"Paul is coming, and he's calling Alan too."

"That's fine. But what I am going to do about the groceries? Plus I need to call Kathy to let her know what's going on. She's watching the boys."

"You can put the cold stuff in our refrigerator for now."

"That'll work. Thanks so much, Mom." I hugged her.

I wanted to be home with Hunter and Colt, but I was thankful for my family being there when I needed them. I could've easily been stranded on the highway in the middle of nowhere. After poking around under the Jimmy's hood, my big brothers found the problem: the alternator.

Alan bought a new one from the auto parts store. I can still picture them, Alan with his stocky frame and brown hair, and Paul with his lanky five-foot-eleven frame and dark hair, leaning over the front of the vehicle. Once Paul removed the last stubborn bolt, the new alternator was installed. By flashlight, both of them slaved late into the night to replace the part.

The whole time, I occupied myself the best I could. I either caught up on the latest news with my mom and dad, called Kathy periodically to check on the boys' status, or I rested on the couch. Finally at 2:30 the next morning, my heroes of the night, Paul and Alan, finished the job.

Because they were my brothers, they did not charge any fees, except for aggravation fees! Ha! Funny guys, but boy was I grateful for them. I was speechless as I pondered what God had done. He never let me down. When I had time to process the two events, Colt walking the highway and my car just barely making it to a safe haven at my parent's home, I praised God for His goodness.

"Dear Father,

Thank You for protecting Colt and me! What happened to Destiny could've happened to Colt. I could've broken down in a remote place. Thank You for sending others to our aide. By Your grace, You kept both of us safe. In the form of strangers and family, You sent guardian angels to watch over us.

You must feel the same way about me as I do about the boys. When You see me making decisions that may cause me harm or if I'm about to enter into not so favorable situa-tion, You rescue me and my loved ones. Sometimes I don't realize my mistake until it's too late, while other times I know better and still do it. Please forgive me for my carelessness. I'm sorry.

No matter what I do, You watch out for all of my family. That gives me a peace of mind. Please continue to keep us safe and help me not to worry about our lives. They are in Your hands. In Jesus' name. Amen."

CHAPTER TEN

FINDING MY PURPOSE

"The days of the blameless are known to the LORD, and their inheritance will endure forever. In times of disaster they will not wither; in days of famine they will enjoy plenty." Psalm 37:18-19

"But the eyes of the LORD are on those who fear him, on those whose hope is in his unfailing love, to deliver them from death and keep them alive in famine."
Psalm 33:18-19

Having asked God to help me not worry about my life, knowing He had it all under control, you would think I could feel more settled in my job. However, the weather and my health issues required me to miss work at times, and I had to put in extra hours and long days. The good news was that I received a pay raise! The bad news was that my stress levels and blood pressure increased more and more by the day.

"You are letting the class get out of control," a fellow teacher accused me one day.

One incident nearly brought me to the breaking point. I needed to attend a parent meeting one afternoon and my supervisor had asked a fellow teacher to remain with the kids while I went to the meeting. Unfortunately the room was chaotic and I misunderstood who was staying and who was going. I answered with an exasperated, and yes, maybe sarcastic retort. The next thing I knew, I was being written up for insubordination. I admitted my fault, and I understood why I was receiving the reprimand, but it only added to the job stress I was dealing with.

Lord, I'm begging you to change the situation at work. I'm desperate here. Other than Danny, I have no one in which to confide in or express my worries who will care to listen. Danny won't listen to me anymore because he's tired of hearing me complain all the time. And poor Hunter and Colt. I'm yelling at them too much. I wish Lareesa was here, but she is a thousand miles away.

On a positive note, my job was ever changing. When Hunter and Colt moved to their new classrooms, I moved back to teaching the two- and three-year-olds. I was ready for the change since the three- to five-year-old classroom caused me to question my ability as a teacher. Even the new three- to five-year-old teacher, the one who had ridiculed my own classroom management skills, admitted the difficulty she had in managing the group. I couldn't pinpoint the reasons for the

problems in that classroom, but I relaxed in my new environ-
ment with the younger children and I began liking my job
again. I received an award for working at the learning center
for three years at the company picnic.

When I started my fourth year there, I had been assigned to
teach the one-year-olds for the new program year. I believed
I had found my niche as a teacher and felt good about my
abilities, until that September.

> *"My teaching career is over. Ten years gone.*
> *Why? I was fired. An eighteen-month-old bit*
> *a three-month-old while I was cleaning the*
> *diaper changing area. My back was turned to*
> *them and every few moments I would glance*
> *over my shoulder. I did not witness the toddler*
> *bite the infant, but I saw him hit her. I hurried*
> *over to them, finally noticing the bite marks.*
> *I felt horrible! I wrote up an incident report*
> *and discussed what happened with the other*
> *teacher on duty and my supervisor. The infant*
> *had calmed down by then, and I went home*
> *thinking everything would be okay. The next*
> *day, however, the director of the center, and*
> *my supervisor, called me into the office and*
> *informed me that the infant had been taken*
> *to the ER because one of the bite marks had*
> *broken the skin. She had been given antibiotics*

*to avoid infection. In addition, a hotline call
was made on me, therefore placing me under
investigation. I am going to consult a lawyer
so I know about my rights."* -Journal Entry

I wrote out a statement for the investigator, and even though I would never allow a child to injure another child on purpose, I knew my career as a teacher was finished, no matter the outcome of the investigation. I could not bring myself into another classroom to instruct young children again. I questioned my ability as a mom too.

Should I be trusted with my own children? Why did I not see what happened? Why did I not respond quicker?

Although the charges were dismissed, teaching children was no longer a career option in my eyes. What to do? I checked into different places, turned in my resume and answered questions during interviews. None of the jobs lined up with my skills and interests. I considered working for the postal service as a clerk but those positions are difficult to find.

The money I earned for completing Alan's paperwork was not sufficient to keep our bills paid once my unemployment benefits ended. Danny had just switched jobs that summer to work full-time for the Army National Guard, which paid well but not enough that I didn't need a job as well. Of course I believed that God had bigger plans for me but as 2007 came to a close, I wondered what God *did* have planned for me.

Should Danny and I keep pursuing the <u>Financial Peace University</u> course by Dave Ramsey at our church? Would it make a difference at this point?

A few days before Christmas, Danny asked me to talk with him. I detected a serious tone in his voice.

Uh oh. What is it?

I checked on Hunter and Colt who were munching on crackers and drinking juice in the kitchen.

They should be okay while Danny and I discuss this important news, whatever it is.

I sat on the couch so I could see the boys. Danny stood, off to my left, too nervous to sit. I looked up at him.

"Is it good or bad?" I wanted to be prepared to respond either way, although I sensed the news would be the latter.

"I've been picked to go on a deployment to Kosovo for a year. I leave in March."

"To Kosovo? Why? What about Iraq?"

"It's a peacekeeping mission in Kosovo, and it's better than going to Iraq."

"That's true, but a whole year? What am I going to do here?" I cried. Hunter and Colt remained in the kitchen even though they had finished their afternoon snack. They obviously didn't want to get in the middle of the discussion. I'm sure they were thinking Mommy and Daddy were nuts, saying all those strange words, such as "deployment" and "Kosovo."

"Well, you could probably not work at all and just stay home, like you have always wanted. The pay is more than my regular job," Danny said.

"You know, you're right. My unemployment benefits end in March. That'll be perfect timing!" I paused to take it in. "And I can stay home. I can't believe it. God never ceases to amaze me."

I knew the deployment would push me to my limit, however, I also knew this was God's plan. I had peace. The next year, 2008, was going to be a big year. How would I do when the time actually came for Danny to step off American soil and help prevent conflict in a foreign country? Only God knew. But there was one important benefit to the lengthy separation-getting our finances back on track.

During our financial hardship, Danny and I made it through only because we received support from coworkers, family, and friends. God had used other people to help us along the way as He always did, yet I had still felt there was no one who cared about us!

In times of famine, God had not failed to provide our needs. He didn't do it in the way I had planned or thought of in my own mind. His plans were not clear at first but I knew He loved me enough to use my weakest moments as ways to strengthen me. He kept his promise in Jeremiah 29:11, which says, "For I know the plans I have for you," declares the Lord, "plans to prosper you and not to harm you, plans to give you a hope and a future."

Even when His plans may not be fulfilled perfectly because I mess them up, they always seem to prevail, despite my mistakes or harmful intentions of others.

"Dear Heavenly Father,

Other people's words and actions, as right as they may have been at the time, almost destroyed my reputation. How awful I felt as a person! Thank You for restoring my self-worth, and thank You for answering my prayer to be a Stay-at-Home-Mom. It didn't happen in the way I had thought. I believed I would find a part-time job from home or Danny's income would increase somehow with his permanent job. I never imagined it would happen from Danny going on a deployment or that I would be accused of child neglect in the process.

At least I had You, my family, and friends to help me through this ordeal, just in time to enjoy the celebration of your Son's birth! I am finally on my way to finding my purpose. I don't know all that I am supposed to do, but You will show me in time. For now, I will stay home with Hunter and Colt as our soldier serves overseas for a year. Please give me strength to get through this. Give me peace. In Jesus' name. Amen."

CHAPTER ELEVEN

SAYING GOODBYE

~∞~

"So do not fear, for I am with you; do not be dismayed,
for I am your God. I will strengthen you and help
you; I will uphold you with my righteous right hand."
Isaiah 41:10

"Peace I leave with you; my peace I give you. I do not
give to you as the world gives. Do not let your hearts be
troubled and do not be afraid." John 14:27

"I can do everything through him who gives me
strength." Philippians 4:13

When 2008 began, I spent my days finishing paperwork for Alan and preparing for the upcoming deployment. Danny obtained his passport, and I picked up my military I.D. We also did maintenance on our vehicles, filed our taxes, and bought Danny new clothes and glasses. Danny assigned me to be Power of Attorney.

Danny and I spent as much time together as possible. We sought out a photographer who took family pictures. I took more pictures of Danny and the boys to add to the family album. The boys and I would at least have those memoirs to help us feel close to Danny when he was thousands of miles from home. Alan offered to purchase a laptop with a webcam for Danny so we could video chat as well.

In the midst of all these last minute details to tend to, Danny and I encountered a fright when Preacher (real name Donald), Danny's dad, had a mini-stroke and was admitted into the hospital. He was confused about the location of his bed and did not know the year.

Although Preacher recovered from his stroke, I was worried about the health for both of Danny's parents while he was away. They both had health issues that required extra care on occasion. Thinking about them and the numerous responsibilities I had to take on overwhelmed me. Staying busy? Not a problem for me! Not only did I have the normal activities to keep up with, I had a house to repair and Danny's parents to look after.

On the night of Hunter's birthday, I sat on the couch in the living room, writing in my journal and watching my favorite show at the time, "CSI: Miami," while Danny tucked the boys into bed. I reflected on the day. The family had romped around in the family fun center, Planet Fun, and had shopped at Toys R' Us. Lots of exciting times to go around.

I also reflected back on the past four years as Hunter's mom. The ups and downs changed us both, and he was growing up. The ear infections had finally quit and he toughed it out for his shots at his checkup. No tears. He was a big boy now. He used the bathroom on his own and stayed dry all night. I wrote this note to him in my journal:

> *"Happy Birthday Hunter! I love you. You may not be a baby anymore but you are still my "Little Sugars."*

As I wrote this entry, the house started shaking. *TORNADO!*

The weather had been unseasonably warm, and storms were in the forecast, but there were no tornado watches or warnings for the area. I jumped off the couch and ran to the boys' room.

"Danny! Get the boys! I think it's a tornado!" I screamed at him above the wind.

"Hunter, Colt. Come here with Daddy," Danny ordered, grabbing their blankets. We had no time to go outside to the basement door.

The boys acted more amused than scared as we huddled in the hallway. They giggled under their blankets. My heart pounded in my chest and my eyes widened with fear, as always expecting the worst. The violent storm passed quickly, thank goodness, but what a sight to see in our yard! The hail looked as if an inch of snow had fallen, and the roof was missing shingles. As far as we could guess in the darkness of the night, only our roof sustained major damage. A couple of days later, our insurance adjuster examined the property and disagreed.

"Your roof, siding, gutters, window sills, screens, deck, barn, and chicken coop will all need fixing or replaced. The estimated total cost of damage is $11,600," he informed us.

$11,600!?

"This much damage came from straight winds? It really sounded like a tornado," I said with certainty.

I considered what could have happened that night. Even though we had experienced a frightful moment and our home needed some TLC, we were safe and together.

When March came, the reality of Danny having to leave on the 18th crushed me like a ton of bricks. I wept off and on when no one was looking.

"Daddy, I'll miss you when you go to Kosovo," Hunter told his Daddy.

Those words broke my heart. I tried to hide my pain, especially for the two "going away" parties hosted by the church and our family on the weekend before his departure.

To complicate the situation, Colt's little nose ran nonstop and his temperature reached 102 degrees Fahrenheit. I had to stay inside with him during the family's party at our house. It was held in our garage, which was detached from the house and definitely not a place for a sick child to be with the rain and cold.

"Why doesn't anyone offer to watch Colt so I can be out there? Yet, I'm not sure I want to be out there after what Kathy said. She had the nerve to say our garage is messy. I get it, sort of. She wants the best for her son who she won't see for a year, but she has to understand that no one in the family volunteered to help me move anything. Probably didn't think about it. Since this party was a surprise, I couldn't ask Danny or he would've questioned me as to why I wanted to rearrange everything. This was his family's idea but I did the work and can't even go to the party!"

I crossed my arms and peered out the window toward the garage. "It's not fair! I am always stuck inside with the kids while the other adults get to socialize. I am always left out!" I pouted. It didn't occur to me that I was acting like a child. If it had, I wouldn't have cared.

The following Monday after the parties, on the 17th, just one day before Danny left, we both waited in the doctor's office with Colt.

"Colt has pneumonia. The good thing is you caught it early enough so it's not severe. There's no need for hospitalization. What he will need is to be on breathing treatments every four hours, and take a steroid for his lungs. He should get better within a couple of days. If he does happen to get worse, please call me," the doctor instructed us.

Lord, I hope this is not a sign of what is to come. Saying goodbye to the love of my life is difficult enough without the added stress of nursing a sick child back to health.

The one comfort I had that day rested in the knowledge of people praying for us. They were our saving grace. Not to mention, Danny would be back home on leave in a few days. I crossed the days off on the calendar. I told myself with each day that passed, was one day closer to the end of the deployment. The beginning was the hardest.

On March 22nd, I woke up early to get ready for the Departure Ceremony. A friend of mine babysat the boys for me. She took them to two Easter Egg Hunts.

Kathy rode with me to the ceremony. It was nice enough but I was anxious to see Danny. I had missed him so much. He was only staying for the weekend to celebrate Easter. While he was home, we were obligated to spend time with our families; however, we squeezed in a few precious moments together.

The boys and I returned Danny back to his unit the next day. The boys surveyed the busses as they slowly rolled by, and I pointed out the one Danny was in.

"He's right there boys! Wave!" I tried to smile through the tears. I reminded myself that he would be home again in two and a half weeks, just in time for his birthday.

While we waited for our beloved hero, the boys and I blew bubbles, drew with sidewalk chalk, played baseball, and rode bikes. Anything to keep us occupied. Hunter learned to pedal his bike on his own and shared his exciting news with everyone we met. He completed a preschool screening through the school and scored well overall.

The boys and I went to church for the first time without Danny. I listened to the service alone, which I wasn't used to, but I needed to be there. Fellowship with my church family was important. I needed their support just as I did from my family and friends. I was gradually adjusting to Danny being gone, and knew I would be okay.

For Danny's next temporary release from service, I had to sit with him through some briefings on retirement, insurance, and the family handbook. The information had to be covered, but I was more than ready to pick up the boys from daycare and spend time together as a family.

At our church, the congregation prayed for us and then we said hello to Danny's family. We snuck away for a date to celebrate his birthday. When the time came for the boys and me to take Danny back to the base, we were expected to attend another departure ceremony.

"Hunter, come on! We have to go for the ceremony!" I urged him.

We had just eaten breakfast in the mess hall and were headed to the gym. The rest of us were already walking in that direction. To catch up, Hunter raced around the corner where he hit the open end of a metal buffet bar. The force knocked him flat on his back. He scrambled up and jogged over to Danny, who gave him a hug.

I spotted drops of blood on the floor.

"Danny, he's bleeding!"

"What?"

"He's bleeding!" I shouted even louder. I had to frequently repeat myself when talking with him because he suffered hearing loss while serving in the Marines as a young adult.

Danny pulled Hunter away from him to see his face covered in blood. Different people hurried to the bathroom and came back with paper towels. Colt bawled hysterically, and I tried to soothe him. He was more upset than Hunter.

Danny's uniform was stained red all down the front. We located the source of the bleeding from Hunter's forehead, which had been cut from the buffet bar.

"Can't the nurse treat him?" I insisted, searching for someone to come to our aide.

"He's not on the insurance here. You'll have to take him to the hospital," another soldier replied.

"Come on Hunter. Mommy and Daddy have to take you to the emergency room."

The hospital was only a few minutes from the base. Hunter started getting sleepy on the drive there.

"Danny, we need to hurry up. He's starting to go to sleep."

"I'm going as fast as I can, Lisa!"

"I know."

At the ER, the nurse and doctor acted quickly. They sowed three stitches in Hunter's forehead and handed us after care instructions. Hunter had also suffered a mild concussion.

93

If this keeps happening, I am going to lose my mind! First Colt, now Hunter. What next? Things have got to get better!

I dropped Danny off in time to board the bus. His unit had waited for him. I prayed, as I did periodically, that God would keep all of us safe. The next eleven months stretched ahead like an eternity. How would I make it through?

My doubts faded for a short time when Danny left his call of duty one last time from May 2nd to May 5th. Once again, we visited family and attended church together. At the park, Danny barbecued hot dogs and hamburgers. Both of us played with the boys. I captured some of our antics on film for our deployment album.

Danny and I went on our "last" date, and then all too sudden, we were forced to say our long goodbyes.

"I don't want you to go! I don't think I can do this!" I sobbed into his shirt.

"You will be okay, Lisa, I promise. I will call you when I get to Indiana. This will go by faster than you think. I love you so much." He held me close, not wanting to go either.

"I know, but it feels like forever! I love you too...I will miss you."

"I will miss you too." He slowly let me go and climbed into the car with the other men. They drove away. I stood there watching the car until I could see it no more. My heart ached and my stomach twisted in knots.

As soon as the car disappeared out of sight, I stopped by to talk with a close friend for a while. She was alone too, and

I thought we could comfort each other. Her husband died six months earlier and I knew she would understand how bereft I felt. A moment later, though, I focused on the difference in our situations.

You know, even though Danny will be five thousand miles away, I can still see him on the web cam, talk to him on the phone, and email him letters whenever I want. He is still with me, unlike my friend, whose husband is gone forever, at least from this world. It's like the pastor said in one of his recent sermons, "Nothing lasts forever, look to God, and ask for help. Rely on His Word."

"Dear Father,

I don't know how I am going to survive these next ten months, but You do. I need You and with You I will do this. I am not strong enough on my own. With Your help, I will ask for what I need and depend on the people You send me. Please give me peace and strength. Give me the wisdom I need. Thank You for my support system and for Your presence near me. I know I am not alone even if I feel alone. I want to enjoy the boys as much as I can. I don't want stress to overcome me. I have to tell myself I can be imperfect. I don't have to do it all myself! Renew my hope. In Jesus' name. Amen"

CHAPTER TWELVE

A TIME TO LIVE AND A TIME TO DIE

"There is a time for everything, and a season for every activity under heaven: a time to be born and a time to die...a time to weep and a time to laugh, a time to mourn and a time to dance..." Ecclesiastes 3:1-2a, 4

Since Danny was absent, I had to play his role on occasion. With the boys in tow, I visited both our dads on Father's Day and snapped a few pictures of them with the grand kids. I cannot express how grateful I was to have taken those photos. They turned out to be priceless keepsakes.

Preacher's health failed more every day. He had cirrhosis of the liver from using pain medication long term, and the doctors suspected he had stomach cancer too. They couldn't say for sure because Preacher was too sick to be tested. His blood pressure and heart rate fluctuated as fluid built up in his abdomen. He had already suffered a mini-stroke that caused brief confusion.

His time on earth was uncertain, unless God performed a miracle. In spite of Kathy's wishes to keep the situation a secret from Danny, I updated him as much as possible. I understand Kathy not wanting her youngest son to worry when he served his country overseas, but he had a right to know. Plus, he had the opportunity to tell his commander about his father's condition so he could be sent home if necessary.

Preacher was quite sick, but he mustered enough strength to attend Colt's third birthday party in mid-July. He did not feel well and asked to lie down on our bed. One of my friends took a picture of him as he stood up next to Kathy. Another moment to cherish.

While Preacher rested, the other guests watched Colt open his presents and eat his Diego birthday cake. He was old enough to fully appreciate the gifts–a John Deere dump truck, a bulldozer, a race car, Legos, a Diego rescue pack, clothes, a movie, a drawing pad, coloring book and crayons. He definitely enjoyed his special day. I could not believe he was a preschooler!

As we had feared, Preacher had to be admitted into the hospital a few days after Colt's party, and then to a nursing home. I will never forget the way he looked and acted that Friday when the boys and I visited him at the facility. His snowy beard had been shaved. The life had gone out of his eyes and he could barely hold his fork to eat. His skin had yellowed from the jaundice. His belly bulged out from the accumulation of fluid, while at the same time he had lost weight over the rest of his body. The skin sagged on his larger-than-average build.

Kathy cheerfully discussed future plans with him of what he would do once he returned home. Maybe she did not see the signs, or she was in denial. Either way, I sensed the end was near. That following Sunday morning, Mike called me.

"Hello, Lisa?" Mike said, taking deep breaths to get the words out.

"Yes."

"I think you need to call for Danny to come home. Dad's in the emergency room. The doctor said his organs are shutting down."

"Oh no! I'll call the American Red Cross and let them know."

I suspected this day would come soon, so I had planned on calling the American Red Cross that following Monday. However, with Preacher being in critical condition, I could no longer wait. I tried reaching the local personnel and no one answered.

I bet they are at church. What am I going to do? Call the main number?

Much to my relief, I reached a sympathetic gentleman at the main office. He agreed to take Danny's case.

I wanted to call Danny but all I could was email him, hoping he read the message. All morning I kept glancing at my phone, praying for it to ring with him on the other end.

Come on Danny, please call. I need to talk to you!

"Mommy! Hunter pushed me down," Colt said to me. I had been standing close to the kitchen counter where I had set my phone.

"Hunter, why did you push Colt down?" I asked, looking at him from the kitchen, hands on my hips.

"He knocked down my tower," Hunter said.

"Is that true?" I asked Colt.

"Yeah."

That boy of mine was sure sneaky. He constantly tried to get his big brother in trouble.

"Colt, tell Hunter you're sorry and help him fix it." I said. "That's not very nice."

"Sowwy Huntew," Colt said, hugging him.

"No you're not!" Hunter shouted, removing Colt's arms off his shoulders.

Riiiiiiiiing!

Danny's number lit up the screen on my phone.

Yes! Thank you, Lord!

"Hello dear," I answered. "Did you get my email?"

He hadn't seen it.

The boys were still arguing, and I held my finger to my lips to hush them. They stared at me for a few seconds and went back to playing. Hunter rebuilt his tower of blocks while

Colt found his new race car and pushed it back and forth on the carpet.

"Your dad is in the hospital. Mike called me earlier this morning. The doctor said your dad's organs are shutting down. It doesn't sound good. Remember when I told you he didn't look good last Friday?"

"Yeah, I remember that. Does Mike think I should come home?" His voice wavered.

"I already called the American Red Cross. You should hear from them soon."

"I haven't yet...wait a minute. My commander wants to speak with me." I could hear muffled voices in the background.

"I need to go. They got my emergency leave ready. I'll call you later. Thank you for doing that. You're the best. I'll see you soon."

"Okay, and Danny? I'm so sorry about your dad. I'll be praying for you to make it safely so you can say goodbye. Be careful coming home."

"I will."

"I love you."

"I love you, too."

Danny flew out from Kosovo that afternoon our time. The American Red Cross was quick to send Danny home on emergency leave, but unfortunately he was forced to stay in Austria for a twenty-six hour layover. How nerve racking! He had nothing to do but think about his dad. I prayed the whole time that he would make it home before Preacher slipped into a coma or departed from this world. Our church prayed too.

Late Tuesday evening, July 29th, Danny's plane arrived at Lambert Airport. The boys and I picked him up. We hastily said our hellos and whisked him away to the hospital.

Preacher was awake and alert when Danny walked into the room. His eyes brightened.

"Hey, Preacher! Who's that?" Kathy asked.

"That's Daniel Joseph Weitkamp," he replied, grinning.

Everyone else smiled. What a sweet moment! I could not thank God enough, especially considering the fact that Preacher fell into a coma the next day.

The family gathered by his bedside as his last breaths quietly left his body. "Preacher, it's okay for you to go. We will be fine here," everyone said.

I took his hand. *Lord, please take him. He's ready.*

I choked back a tear.

We stood silently as one of Preacher's own tears trickled out of his eyes as if to say goodbye. There were no machines. He left peacefully, just as he had requested.

He must have heard us tell him he could go. He took his Father's hand and crossed over to the other side. I envisioned him running with the angels and with his loved ones who had died before him. He was home. The day: July 31, 2008.

The family comforted each other that evening. We cried on each other's shoulders, grieving the loss of a wonderful man. Sobs coursed through Danny's body. It was rare for him to show emotion, but even he could not hide the pain. The days to follow were blurry and surreal. What impacted me most was the number of people who came to offer their condolences.

"Look at that line of people who keep coming in!" I commented, observing them through a small window in the children's room downstairs.

I had to keep an eye on Hunter and Colt for part of the visitation until they left to play with their cousin. The funeral director estimated about five hundred people to stop by, paying their last respects! This was a significant number of visitors considering Preacher lived in a small town of about ten thousand residents. The funeral director had to print off more obituary cards.

I'm in awe. Preacher really made a difference in so many lives. I want to be like him someday, helping people like he did.

"Is Grandpa in heaven Mommy?" Hunter asked, tugging on my shirt.

"Yes he is. His spirit went there. His old body is what you see in the casket." Hunter redirected his attention toward the casket.

"Where is heaven?"

"I don't know for sure, but it's a really nice place. God is there, and Grandpa is not sick anymore. He can walk without a cane now. Isn't that great?"

"Yeah. I miss him though."

"Me too, Bub. We all do."

The boys did not attend the funeral. The hot temperatures kept other people from going to the graveside service. Since Mike worked for the fire department full-time, they led the procession out to the cemetery. My heart swelled with pride for this man, my father-in-law, whose body was being laid to rest that day. He would continue to live in our thoughts and in future generations.

I vowed to share his stories with his grandchildren. We sorted through old pictures and looked at more recent ones, such as the one on Father's Day and the one at Colt's party. Kathy, John (Danny's other big brother who could almost be his twin), Mike, and Danny reminisced about his love of the lottery, gardening, and tractors. And oh how he adored his grandchildren!

In the days to follow, Danny and I helped his mom sort through cards and plants. The family received about twenty plants, two of which found a home with us. We also finished some household tasks, vehicle maintenance and yard work.

Before Danny returned to Kosovo on August 13th, we enjoyed family time with fishing, swimming, and a barbecue. For Danny's and my eighth anniversary, we watched a movie and visited a local winery. I could feel the love surrounding us.

"You know I'm not using birth control," I reminded Danny. We relaxed outside on the patio with a bottle of wine.

"Yeah, I know," he replied. "I'm not worried about it. I think you want another one, don't you?"

"I don't know. Maybe."

"We'll see what happens."

Just a week after Danny returned to Kosovo, I took a home pregnancy test. As I expected, two pink lines showed up. To think at one time I'd wondered if I'd ever be able to get pregnant, now I had learned to trust God's timing. Life had come from death.

"Hey, Danny. Guess what?" I exclaimed to him later that day on the phone. I stood outside on the sidewalk. The boys were swinging and the sun shone warm and bright.

"I have no idea. Did the yard get mowed?" he joked.

"No! I took a pregnancy test and I am pregnant!"

"Are you serious? I didn't think you would get pregnant so fast."

"Danny, don't you remember how quickly I became pregnant with Colt?" I gestured toward the sky with my hand.

"Well yeah, but I didn't expect it to happen again."

"You aren't disappointed are you?" I asked.

I hope he's not upset.

"No! I didn't mean that. I'm happy. Are you?" he wanted to know.

"Oh yeah! And if the baby is a boy, I am naming him Donald Joseph, after you and your dad. What do you think?"

"That would be great. Mom will like that. There's no doubt the baby will be a boy. I am all man. I can't produce a girl."

"Ha! Ha! We will see," I rolled my eyes. "As long as the baby is healthy, that's all that matters to me."

"Me too," Danny agreed.

"Oh and Danny?"

"Yes?"

"Thanks for getting me pregnant and leaving me!" I laughed.

By this time, Danny had returned to Kosovo. Alan had driven the boys and me to the airport. I did not cry as much this time when my soldier walked further down the terminal, away from me. He would return home in about three months for Thanksgiving. Besides, I had to focus on the job ahead of me. I had three kids to care for- the two little ones running around and the one growing in my belly.

"Dear Lord,

Thank You for Preacher's time on this earth. I feel honored to have known him. He really made a big impact on people in the community. He left the kind of legacy that I want to leave, of helping people. I haven't been very good at that. Neither have I been good at asking for help. I don't want to bother people, and I'm concerned about getting my own things done. I don't want to be like that anymore. Maybe if I reached out to other people more, they would be there for me and I wouldn't feel guilty about it. Thank You for revealing this truth to me. Please forgive me. In Jesus' name. Amen."

CHAPTER THIRTEEN

FACING LIFE ALONE DURING DEPLOYMENT

≈

"Be joyful in hope, patient in affliction, faithful in
prayer." Romans 12:12

"Consider it pure joy, my brothers, whenever you face
trials of many kinds..." James 1:2

Before Danny left for Kosovo, I carefully built my support group from church, family, and friends, knowing how hard it was for me to ask for help. I also created goals for myself to lose weight, visit family often, assemble my favorite puzzles, take the boys out on new adventures, and read new books.

Even so, all the chores needing to be done weighed me down. Anxiety and depression were no strangers to me that spring. Paxil eased my symptoms, but did nothing to find people to help me.

Where are all the people who said to let them know if I needed anything? They seemed to have disappeared.

Constant rain made progress slow. The roof needed new shingles and the grass had grown several inches high. In addition, the Jimmy's right wheel hub broke, a five hundred dollar repair, including labor.

"Can I catch a break soon?" I asked God.

In no time at all, He answered my prayer with sunny skies, family and friends tending to my needs, and projects being completed. The grass was mowed, the Jimmy was fixed, the new shingles were put on, and both the septic tank and A/C vents were cleaned out.

The boys and I started a new tradition of buying lunch at McDonald's and eating at the park every Wednesday, at least during the summer. At home we watched cartoons on our satellite TV and created art with glue, scissors, and crayons. The boys' favorite creation was the ooblick! (Think play dough that is ooey gooey.)

For Father's Day, we had to plan early. Mail traveled slower across the globe. About the time we celebrated the special day, Danny had officially arrived in Kosovo. Along with movies, pictures, and a list of why he was a great daddy, Hunter and Colt sent handmade cards to their hero. Danny valued any item from home.

By the time summer was in full swing, the boys and I had settled into our new routine, and I was finally at peace. No more crying or feelings of despair. God had helped me be strong enough to endure each day. I felt confident. I knew I was going to be okay with Him by my side.

I also changed our internet service from dial-up to an air card. The kids and I loved to see Danny on the webcam! He was seven hours ahead of us so we talked to him late in the morning or early afternoon. There were also emails:

Dear Lisa, Hunter, and Colt:

Just wanted to say hi and I love you all. I sure do miss you a lot. I look forward to seeing your faces and hearing your voices. I hope the weather is good back there so you can go outside and play or go to the park. I think of you guys often and I look at the pictures every night when I go to bed and when I wake. I LOVE YOU ALWAYS DADDY, Danny.

Danny,

Hello to you too. I miss you, love you, and I definitely can't wait to see you!!! I have been dreaming about you. In one dream you came home for a surprise visit. Have you been

dreaming of me and what kind of dreams? I have been fixing up the house. You will think you have a new house when you come home! Don't worry, you'll still have the same little wife and kids. I do hope you are doing okay. I am okay. The house and kids are keeping me busy. I mark off every day on the calendar that passes. One day closer to seeing you. Well, I better go. Happy Father's Day! Talk to you tomorrow I hope.
With hugs, kisses, and lots of love,
Lisa

Lisa,

I read your E-mail and it made me happy to hear about your dreams and that I am in them. You are all a dream come true and I am blessed beyond words. With you and the boys, I feel like the richest man on earth. I miss you dearly with us being apart. I really realize how much I love you and depend on you and I know I didn't tell you that much back home. I am sorry. You and the boys are the most important thing in the world to me. I am living a dream of being your husband and

long for the day until I hold you again. Give
the boys a hug for me. I LOVE YOU.
Danny

Shortly after Danny departed in May, I wrote "47 weeks until deployment is over! 329 days and 10 1/2 months."

Was I counting? Of course! Ha! Ha! At least I knew I had plenty of time to reach my goals and practice patience. I was dependent on other people then, and they sacrificed their time and energy to help me. I grew closer to them and learned to say "Thank you" more often. I stepped out of my comfort zone too, doing things I wouldn't normally do, like taking care of the vehicles and the yard. I had let Danny take care of all of that in the past.

By August, the house was fixed, and I became busy with other tasks. Alan had asked me to become his dispatcher. Not only would I be in charge of the paperwork, I would also find loads needing transport for him. Being a dispatcher was all new to me and learning the tasks proved to be more challenging than I first thought, especially since I had to care for two young boys and keep the home front in order, all while being pregnant. I was exhausted! I had already lost twenty-five pounds that year, and I lost a few more pounds during my first trimester. Stress was my constant companion.

Here's what I wrote one day:

"At least the weather is calm, unlike my life. One thing after another, major things. First my job, then the hail storm,

then Danny goes on Deployment, Preacher gets sick and dies, then the pregnancy. Some good, some bad. Overall good in the end, but man, can things settle down for a change?"

My life seemed to be in a constant whirlwind. All I wanted was normalcy.

Danny felt guilty for leaving me pregnant. I assured him I was fine. I had founds ways to maintain my sanity by focusing on the events that brought peace and calm. One new change included Hunter starting preschool. Although he performed within normal limits on the screening, he scored below average in his fine motor skills (he hated coloring, writing, and cutting) and social skills. The district's Title I Preschool program opened up a spot for him in the morning session. I seized the opportunity!

I almost cried when I put him on the bus, though. My Little Bub was in school. He loved it too, except for the fine motor activities. He told the teachers that Colt aggravated him. They were impressed with his vocabulary. At just two-years-old, he had memorized the <u>Freight Train</u> by Donald Crews.

I was grateful Hunter had been given a chance to maintain his strong skills and improve on his weaker ones at the same time. I felt assured that he would be ready for kindergarten the next year.

As for Colt, he played alone and watched TV while I called brokers and faxed information to them. I sensed that he felt lost without Hunter. He missed his daddy, too. He lacked attention and tested my patience with his behavior.

He refused to master toilet training and he was sure stubborn. Not only that, he aggravated Hunter constantly. Hunter had told his teachers the truth about that.

I signed Colt up for story hour at the library where he listened to stories and created art projects. I hoped the interaction with same age peers would help him feel better. He could at least have this special time to enjoy being with mommy and playing with other kids. His behavior improved. He mastered toilet behavior again. During this time I had also agreed to have his speech tested through the school. I wondered if not being understood by others caused frustration in him as well.

My schedule was full that fall, but I tried to find time for fun with the boys whenever possible. We visited the fire station where Mike worked. We saw the monster truck named Big Foot there. The boys sat in its cab and climbed on its larger than life tires. We also visited the pumpkin patch where Hunter and Colt played in bins full of soybeans, corn, and wheat. They also played in the sand pit, pedaled toy tractors, and rode on a little train.

For Halloween, Hunter dressed up as a Blue Ninja and Colt dressed up as Superman (he insisted he was Spider-Man though!). They trick-or-treated in the neighborhood by Grandma Kathy's house and returned with more than enough candy.

At the end of October, I was feeling optimistic about the deployment. It was more than half over. Danny and I were "seeing" each other on the webcam every week and talking everyday on the phone. I had passed my one year mark of being fired, and I had renewed my faith in God.

I was back to reading the Bible and praying. Without my Father's presence in my life, I was a mess! I felt relaxed most of my days but the dispatching job continued to bring more stress than I could handle.

A week before Danny was due to arrive home on leave again, toward the middle of November, I woke up at about two in the morning to use the bathroom. That's when I saw blood. The word "miscarriage" popped into my head. I freaked out.

"Hello," Alan answered groggily. He was driving to his next delivery.

"Alan! I think I'm having a miscarriage! What should I do?" I asked with panic in my voice. Hunter and Colt were asleep in my bed. I tried not to wake them up. The kitchen, where I sat at the table, was next to the bedroom.

"Oh man, Lisa. Sorry to hear that! Did you call your doctor?"

"No, not yet." I checked to make sure I had her number by the phone.

"What about Kathy? Or Mike?"

"No."

"Why don't you try calling them. If I was home I would help you."

"I know. But I will call my doctor and Mike. Thanks Alan."

113

"Let me know what happens. I hope the baby is okay."

"Me too. I am so scared."

My doctor advised me to go to the ER as soon as possible. I called Kathy who asked my brother-in-law, John, to drive me to the hospital while Kathy stayed at the house with the boys. The drive lasted forty-five minutes but seemed like forty-five hours. John dropped me off at the doors. The receptionist's chair was empty.

Where is everybody? What should I do now?

John walked in followed by a young couple. The young man pushed a wheelchair with his partner in it. He shouted, "Where is a doctor? My girlfriend had a miscarriage yesterday, and she is in pain now!"

She grimaced and held her stomach. The commotion caused people to come running.

Oh Lord, please save my baby.

After wheeling the sick lady off to labor and delivery, a black man in a suit casually approached the desk. He requested my insurance information and motioned me back to a room. John stayed in the waiting room. The nurse warned me about the extended wait time due to an accident, but I didn't think I would be sitting in that room for *six* hours without one doctor checking in on me. I was alone and terrified. The nurse had found the baby's heartbeat, which was strong, but why was I bleeding?

Since the ER doctors refused to provide care, I called my OB/ GYN who was upstairs in the same building. They squeezed me in. The doctor confirmed that I was bleeding and ordered an ultrasound. The placenta was intact and the baby moved inside. The doctor believed I had blood trapped in my uterus before the pregnancy and it was coming out. She assured me that this type of bleeding happens. I wanted to dance.

Thank You, Lord, for saving my baby!

Hunter called his soon-to-be sibling his "favorite baby." He predicted the baby to be a girl. I wished for a girl, too. Even though I had the ultrasound, the baby was not developed enough for the gender to be determined.

Both boys handled the baby fright with ease. We did not let that day change our excitement in seeing Danny again. He flew in the 19th of November. We picked him up from the airport. We couldn't find him right away and then, all of a sudden, there he was two feet away. We embraced him in the biggest hugs we could manage. My belly was starting to bulge out so I couldn't squeeze him too much.

For ten days, we celebrated Christmas, Thanksgiving, and being together as a family. Alan gave me time off. He felt guilty for pressuring me to find loads. He blamed himself for what happened with the ER incident. True, even though the job was difficult, the problem could have happened regardless. No one knows for certain.

While Danny was home in November, we visited the doctor again for another ultrasound, but the doctor could not clearly define the gender. Darn! We had to wait until after

Danny returned overseas. Julie, Mike's wife, accompanied me to that appointment. Before the nurse came in, I kept looking at her, wondering what she was thinking.

She is nearly as tall as Mike with light brown hair worn at shoulder length. She wears glasses like most in the family. She and Mike have a son of their own, Dylan, who is a year younger than Hunter. With all the boys in the family, was she hoping for a girl too? I'm sure she wanted a niece.

Upon waiting for the ultrasound, I had convinced myself the baby was a girl. So when the nurse pointed to the white spot on the screen between the baby's legs and asked me if I knew what that was, I reluctantly answered, "A penis."

My displeasure only lasted a few seconds, though. Yay! Another baby boy. Danny was excited to have his Donald Joseph. Maybe he was right when he said he was all man and could not produce a girl.

As the days of December passed, I missed Danny more than ever. My birthday was celebrated without him, but my family and friends called me and sent cards. Kathy treated me to dinner and Danny arranged for flowers to be delivered. My special day actually turned out well despite Hunter wetting my bed that morning. Oh well.

The holidays were more of the same. They emphasized the fact that Danny was gone. Even so, I still made sure the boys enjoyed their Christmas. I somehow managed to lug presents into the house from the car with a big belly. At least the winter weather brought little snow, much to my relief. All

I had to do was bundle up from the cold wind. No worries about slipping on ice or snow.

On Christmas morning, the boys' eyes lit up when they saw the presents under the tree. They tore open their presents from Santa, whom they had visited at the John Deere dealership earlier in the month. They were given a Leapfrog Tag System, an art easel, a Hungry Hippos game, a monster truck, a fire truck, Nerf guns, puzzles, robots, movies, toy cameras, candy canes, and a doctor kit. Danny also opened his presents from us of which we mailed after Thanksgiving. We sent him the Godfather Trilogy and his favorite food, including Oreo cookies and Captain Crunch. He said he had to fight for the cereal!

The holidays ended with another year, and I anticipated what 2009 would be like. Many interesting events awaited me. We were going to meet our third baby boy and Danny's deployment would end. I was going to survive, as hard as it was being alone.

Kathy had found Danny's high school class ring, and I thought back to the first time I wore it. Danny and I had dated while I was in high school. He had been on a tour of duty in the Mediterranean with the Marines. I had placed that ring on my finger as a reminder of his love for me. If I could survive his absence then, I could do it again this time. Even though 2008 was a hard year, God had helped me through.

As 2009 came to be, I thought about my journey into motherhood. By this time, I had accepted the messes, the lack of sleep, and less "me" time. I continued to use my Paxil for the stress and anxiety issues. To most people I handled the single parent status well.

"I don't know how you do it, especially being pregnant," one of my friends admitted.

"My faith in God is what has carried me through." I told her.

Additionally, Danny's love pushed me forward each day until he returned home.

I was looking forward to meeting the new baby, D.J., as we decided to call him. I bought clothes, diapers, bottles, blankets, and toys. I needed everything because I had donated the baby items from Hunter and Colt, believing we were finished having kids.

There I'd be, back to changing diapers, even before Colt became totally toilet trained. No break for me there.

Speaking of breaks, finding a person to keep the boys so I could rest and relax was nearly impossible. People offered to babysit only to excuse themselves later on. They contacted us after the deployment and confessed they had been busy working and spending time with loved ones. Why didn't they just give me that information at the beginning? I was busy too. So busy, in fact, that I did not have time to respond to Lareesa's daily calls and emails. I had to ignore her.

I had another issue to resolve towards the end of the deployment besides finding breaks. I had been summoned for jury duty on the same day I had a doctor's appointment with my OB/GYN. I called the courthouse and the clerk kindly told me I could be dismissed if I had a doctor's note. No big deal right?

"You cannot get out of jury duty because you have an appointment and you are pregnant. It's not a valid medical condition to be excused from jury duty and you can change your appointment." The nurse informed me, sounding disgusted.

Why does she have to be so rude to me? I am alone and pregnant with two young boys while my husband serves our country. What is wrong with her? You would think she would be more understanding and compassionate. I am not trying to get out of jury duty for no good reason.

The only other choice I had was to call the doctor's office back and ask to speak to the doctor himself. He was unavailable at the time of my call so another nurse assured me she would take care of the note. I thanked her, but when I saw the doctor again for my next appointment, I brought up my concerns with him. Displeased with the "mean" nurse, he discussed the situation with everyone at the next staff meeting. A standard letter was devised for pregnant women, who in the future faced a similar circumstance.

I was not shirking my duties strictly for my health. Who would watch the boys while I sat in a courtroom all day? Family lived too far away, and I did not know anyone close by willing and able to carry out such a task. I truly was unable to serve on the jury. I felt that my stand at the doctor's office would help other women in the same situation, so I was honoring Preacher by trying to help others.

For those twelve months of Danny serving his country, I did the best I could on my own. Only by God's grace did I get through one of the most difficult challenges of my life. If there was ever a time when I had to rely on Him, it was then. What a life-changing experience!

"Dear Father,

Thank You for helping me through most of the deployment. I know I cannot survive without You or the people You send me. I need to reach out to others more and step out of my comfort zone. Growth only comes when I push myself to the edge and take that leap of faith in You. I cannot hide in my anxiety and fears. All that does is stop the blessings of true joy. I have to see my problems as opportunities to be more like You, not as opportunities to complain or stress out. Please continue to show me what I need to do so I can have true peace and joy in You. In Jesus' name. Amen."

CHAPTER FOURTEEN

TOGETHER AT LAST?

∾

"Because he loves me," says the LORD, "I will rescue him; I will protect him, for he acknowledges my name. He will call upon me, and I will answer him; I will be with him in trouble, I will deliver him and honor him. With long life I will satisfy him and show him my salvation." Psalm 91:14-16

W hat a relief to put the recent problems behind me, especially when Danny arrived home a week earlier than expected!! HOMECOMING AT LAST! No more marking off the days on the calendar or being alone.

In my journal I wrote:

> *"It was definitely a nice surprise having him come home early. Yep, we'll have things to do and a new baby soon, but there will be*

time to just be together again. We survived the deployment with flying colors. Thank you everyone for all your help and thank You Lord mostly for helping me when times became hard. You gave me strength, comfort, and peace. You helped the time to pass. Now we are together again. We were kept safe and well. Hallelujah!"

We attended church for the first time that year as a complete family. The church members welcomed Danny home with open arms.

We were thrilled to have our soldier home permanently. The boys stayed close to their Daddy, and Colt repeatedly said, "I mist you Daddy. I wuv you." Hunter and Colt both enjoyed being with their Daddy again.

Honestly though, we struggled to gain a new normal after Danny returned home. Accustomed to being alone, Danny hid away to play games on the PSP device.

"Danny?" I called out one day while trying to find him in the house. "Where are you? I could use some help here… What are you doing?" I asked once I found him in the office/playroom. "I've been looking for you. Why do you keep hiding away? Do you just not want to be with us? You seem so distant."

"I'm sorry. I'm used to being alone. But why are you so upset? You stay home all day. You shouldn't need my help."

"Well excuse me!! In case you haven't noticed, I'm eight months pregnant, and I can't do everything that easily. You should be helping me."

He spouted off his usual line of "Women have given birth to babies for centuries and even had to go back out to the fields right away." He also added, "They didn't have help from their husbands or get time off."

"Oh yeah, women have also died because they didn't get the proper care!" I reminded him, fighting back the tears.

I couldn't believe this was my husband talking. What happened to him? Was this how he was going to be? Didn't he love us and hadn't he missed us? Was I going to have to do everything myself?

"Look, I'm sorry," Danny said. "I just wanted to relax a little. I'm not used to all the demands of being home. I'm trying to figure out what to do about money too. Now that I'm back, we'll lose those deployment benefits."

"I'm still working for Alan, don't forget." I placed my hand on his shoulder. As if on cue, Hunter and Colt ran into the room. They wore underwear on their heads and their sleepers were bulging with stuffed animals. Here was a graphic reminder to Danny about what family meant.

"Daddy, what are you doing?" They wanted to know. "Look at us!"

"Oh, not much. You boys are silly!" He tickled them before they escaped, laughing down the hall.

I chuckled at the boys and then turned back to Danny.

"You know dear, I'm worried too, but something will come our way. It always does. We need to trust God. Hasn't He always met our needs?"

"Yes, He has...Thank you for putting up with me," he said, pulling me into his lap. "I don't know what I'd do without you. How did I deserve someone like you? You are so good to me."

He promised to help me more and spend more time with the boys. It was all I wanted to hear.

Despite the hectic schedule, Danny and I eventually found time together as a couple. We went on an actual date. The entire family, all five of us, celebrated Easter and Danny's birthday. That summer, we attended the Yellow Ribbon Event, located at the Marriott Hotel in Kansas City, Missouri. The Yellow Ribbon Event offered child care for soldiers and their spouses as they listened to briefings related to post deployment issues, such as insurance and employment opportunities. We went on two separate occasions: one weekend in June and one weekend in July. Danny signed up for a home inspection course. This prospect offered hope for our finances. Home inspectors can make good money.

Our newborn son, D.J., warmed the hearts of the nursery ladies while the boys played games and created projects within their groups. Danny swam with the two older boys in the hotel pool, and we marveled at the tall buildings while walking downtown after finishing the day's activities. I almost burst with pride as Danny received awards and certificates.

The Yellow Ribbon Event was our family vacation that year. Having that time together, without interruptions, helped us create closer bonds. We weren't preoccupied with getting things done. Instead, we paid attention to each other more. The boys soaked up all the love and affection. It's not that Danny and I completely ignored them, but we hadn't spent a lot of quality time with them. That was going to change.

"I finally feel as if we are together as a family," I told Danny later that summer on our anniversary date. We were hanging out at one of our favorite wineries.

"What do you mean?" he asked.

What had started as a warm feeling in me took a turn. I was dwelling on all the painful parts about Danny's return to us. "We weren't really together, in sync, before now. There was so much going on. We didn't have the time we needed to reconnect. I'm not happy with everyone who wanted you to do stuff for them as soon as you got home. Why didn't they realize we needed family time? They weren't around to visit or help me during the winter and then all of a sudden they showed up when you're home. How rude is that? I know they helped me some here and there, but that doesn't mean we should be there all the time for them." I explained.

"They didn't know. Everything worked out, didn't it?" he reasoned.

"Well, yeah, but still. I wish they had been more considerate. I don't feel as if we had a true homecoming. They stole that from us and we can't get that back. I waited twelve months for that day and it was ruined. It's not fair! They get to do what they want and we don't interfere. Why do they do it to us? Man, people are so clueless!"

"I think you need to let it go. The main thing is that I made it home safely. Not everything can be perfect. And not everyone has a perfect homecoming. Some don't have a homecoming at all. Just remember that."

Sobering thought. Danny was right. Even though our homecoming didn't go as planned or expected in my dreams, we were together. God had kept all of us safe. We were complete as a family again and with one new member, D.J. God's love for us had delivered us from harm and satisfied our desires in His time, not ours.

"Dear Father,

Thank You for keeping us safe while Danny was on his deployment. We survived our time of separation and are now together as a family. It took longer than I expected and it didn't happen the way I wanted, but we are complete again. We have D.J. too! I have a lot to be thankful for, and I shouldn't complain. Continue to help us connect as a family and help Danny fully adjust to being home. While we are doing okay, we still have our issues. Danny has moments where he is not as understanding as he used to be. I'm not sure why. He's getting better, but in the meantime, please reveal to me what I need to do. In Jesus' name. Amen."

CHAPTER FIFTEEN

BIRTHING PAINS

"To the woman he said, 'I will greatly increase your pains in childbearing; with pain you will give birth to children. Your desire will be for your husband, and he will rule over you." Genesis 3:16

"At this my body is racked with pain, pangs seize me, like those of a woman in labor; I am staggered by what I hear, I am bewildered by what I see." Isaiah 21:3

I jumped ahead of myself! I need to tell about the week before D.J. was due to arrive, I felt the pain as if I was already in labor, but I wasn't, at least not yet.

"What in the world?!" I yelled, stumbling into one inch of water on the bathroom floor late one night. "Danny!" The bathroom is flooded! The washing machine is still running. Come here!"

Danny wiped his tired eyes and trudged into the bathroom. He had been asleep, but not once he saw the shocking scene. "What the heck?!" He fumbled around with the machine. "It's the shut off valve. Let me go shut off the water."

"I can't believe this! Of all times! Well, at least we have the Rug Doctor."

Earlier in the day, which happened to be a Saturday, both my parents and Paul had helped Danny and me clean the carpets and rearrange our bedroom to prepare for D.J. His crib had been placed at the foot of our bed, and his dresser sat next to mine. (Space was limited in our 1,050 square foot house.) Danny and I were beyond tired from the work of the day and now we were faced with a flooded bathroom. For the next two days Danny cleaned up water and fixed the washer.

"Man, I'm exhausted," I admitted to Danny as we fell into bed that Monday night.

"You're not kidding!"

"You know, D.J. is moving around kind of funny. I wonder if it's from all the stress."

"Could be." Not being too concerned, I began to fall asleep. Then suddenly I felt wetness in the sheets. "Uh, Danny?" I said. "The sheets are wet."

"The sheets are wet?"

"Yeah."

"Did you leak or something?"

"I don't think so."

"Then what could it be?"

"I think my water broke. This is more than just pee. It keeps coming!"

"Do you want me to call the doctor?"

"Yes, please."

The doctor advised me to come in. Danny and I dropped the boys off with family and quickly drove, without speeding, to the hospital. I kept leaking out fluid on the way there, and after careful examination, the doctor confirmed my water had broken. By the time my registration was completed, it was close to midnight.

The next morning, on Tuesday, April 21st, eight days before his due date, D.J. entered the world weighing 8 pounds, 2 ounces and measuring 21 1/2 inches. The nurses suctioned out his nose and mouth. The doctor told us our little man appeared to be slightly jaundiced and his eyes were full of mucus, but other than that, he was healthy. Praise God!

As I held my new son, I prayed, "Dear Lord, thank You that D.J. is okay, especially with all the scares we had. His kidneys are okay. The placenta moved so I could deliver vaginally. I didn't miscarry and the stress didn't affect his health either. You answered our prayers!"

For the next two days, I enjoyed relaxing and acquainting myself with my "Little Man", while Danny ran back and forth to the hospital and cared for Hunter and Colt. The boys adored their little brother. He was the center of attention at home. We were all devoted to him and didn't even need to cook since two church ladies brought out meals.

Once home, though, I caught myself complaining about watching my nephew, working for Alan, and having to straighten the messy house.

What is wrong with people!? They should be trying to help me ease my burdens, not INCREASE my burdens!

I wasn't getting the help I wanted, and I didn't want to say 'no' to my family because I thought they would accuse me of being selfish. I needed to ask God to give me a cheerful heart when serving others, which never occurred on my schedule or when it was convenient. Saying 'no' was okay, too.

I loved D.J., but our home turned into total chaos! The older boys' behavior worsened to the point where they were fighting more and making more messes. I wasn't eating or sleeping well and Danny would not get up with D.J. unless I pestered him. It's not that D.J. was a difficult baby either. (Except for some spitting up and fussing. His formula had been changed to ease the symptoms.) Danny just didn't seem to realize how much I needed his help.

"God, I could use some help here!" I cried out in desperation.

He answered my prayer, as He always does. Three weeks after being home, I finally slept in and cherished "me" time thanks to Danny. Watching D.J. coo, smile, laugh and blow raspberries lightened my mood, too.

During the days of learning to being a mom of three young boys, I was concerned about working from home, especially since our computer and internet kept crashing. Finding loads for Alan was a nightmare. I accused myself of neglecting the kids to be a dispatcher. Quitting was not an option. We needed the money. Our budget was tight. The deployment income stopped and we had already used our income tax refund money to buy a 2001 Chevy Astro Van and pay bills.

Danny signed up for a home inspector course. Home inspections would bring in extra cash. He passed the course with an eighty-seven percent. We used our credit card to buy items to set up the business. Yes, we were in debt again. I reassured myself that such is life when starting a business, which I hoped would succeed so we could rid ourselves of the chronic money aggravation. Danny's first inspection was that December and I prayed for many more.

Open deer season had begun and Danny shot two deer. He actually got a third deer with our Chevy Aveo (deer crossings....another perk to living in the country). The small car was totaled and we used the extra eight hundred dollars from the insurance to buy an old Ford Ranger. We missed the car in a way, but not the payments. The absence of a vehicle payment certainly eased our financial strain.

To add to all this chaos, the afternoon after we picked up the boys from our anniversary date, we decided to adopt two dogs from the local animal shelter. We named the Jack Russell Terriers Patch and Monty.

What I was thinking? As if the house was not crazy enough, now I had to keep track of the dogs, both of whom were not totally house broken. Worse still, Patch attacked the stray kittens and killed them. I wanted to rip my hair out.

I tried not to feel trapped at home with three kids and two dogs. While I envied people who came and went freely, I had to accept the fact that not everyone got to do what they wanted, and I had to let God's peace reign in the midst of the chaos.

The house eventually calmed down again. The boys started back to school and the dogs ran off with two stray dogs. Whew! I didn't really miss them, but I wanted a dog. We had lost many dogs before them, and I was about to give up when one of Danny's coworkers offered to give us their pug/terrier mix. Tuffy lived indoors and had a laid back personality. We decided to try once again to own a dog. On New Year's Eve we adopted Tuffy. He has been the best dog, and he is still with us as I write this chapter.

When Tuffy came to us that New Year's Eve Day, I felt reassured. I knew my future with three boys and a dog would be exciting and full of adventure. I had nothing to fear, and I thanked God for helping me survive another year.

"Dear Father,

I'm thankful D.J. is okay. He's healthy and so cute! I can't help but love him. I am slowly learning to be a mom of three young boys. May I find my peace in You. Please help me get the rest I need and the help I need. I just have to tell Danny when I want a break and be patient as I wait for it to happen.

Thank You for Tuffy too. I hope he stays with us for a while. I'm tired of losing dogs.

Provide the finances we need to care for the family. May I get more loads for Alan and may Danny get a lot of home inspections. With you by our side, we will be okay. In Jesus' name. Amen."

CHAPTER SIXTEEN

LOVING MY GROWING BOYS

~

"But Jesus called the children to him and said, 'Let
the little children come to me, and do not hinder them,
for the kingdom of God belongs to such as these.'"
Luke 18:16

Back before D.J. was born, a church friend said, "God must think you are good at raising boys to give you three." Danny was still in Kosovo at the time.

"That's for sure!" I agreed, rubbing my pregnant belly.

At the time, I wondered about D.J.'s personality. Would he be funny and smart like Hunter or laid back and observant like Colt? Would he sleep at night? Who would he look like? Regardless, with him and his two older brothers, I would have three Danny Juniors running around!

"I want a WALL-E cake and WALL-E toys!" Hunter, the oldest Danny Junior declared.

I had asked him what he wanted for his fifth birthday. The main item on his list was a transforming WALL-E. I had searched three or four stores for a transforming WALL-E and none of them carried the item, but Danny found the toy online and mailed it to Hunter, along with his own belongings. He had nearly completed his mission in Kosovo. As we celebrated Hunter's birthday, I smiled. No more celebrations without Danny after Valentine's Day.

While I smiled during Hunter's party, I almost cried, too. I couldn't believe he had turned five. Where did the time go? That fall, when he entered kindergarten, tears welled up in my eyes as I drove away from the school. Why did I feel sad? I hadn't lost him and he had succeeded beyond my expectations.

Halfway through the year, his teacher enrolled him in the gifted program. He not only mastered the kindergarten skills but first grade skills too. She named him "Ringmaster", a couple of times as well. ("Ringmaster" was similar to a being a good citizen. Of course he knew how to be a good citizen with Jesus in his heart!)

Hunter accepted Jesus into his heart at Vacation Bible School the summer before kindergarten. What a joy as a mother to witness the salvation of her child. A few months later he was baptized. Being that he was so small, he almost baptized himself as he walked into the water, which nearly reached his head. He was short for his age, but at least by then he had hair, which was brown like the rest of the family.

Before this glorious event, I had prayed, "God, please guide Hunter and protect him all the days of his life. Even if I mess up or become frustrated with him, I know You will intervene," I had prayed. "Show me the reason for his aggression toward Colt and Tuffy. Why is he hitting them and fighting roughly with Colt? Why is he throwing toys and breaking them? He seems angry. Is he upset because he is not getting all the attention? And then there is Colt. What is wrong with him? I know he is unhappy with the situation at home with Daddy gone. I'm busy and stressed out. Is his unruly behavior due to our crazy lives?"

Colt was evaluated by the school for speech and they discovered fluid in his ears. This new discovery explained Colt's speech issues and maybe his behavior. Colt tried to communicate his wants and needs. I could not understand him and he could not hear me clearly either. I scheduled him to be examined by an ENT, who determined Colt needed tubes again. We scheduled the procedure after Danny's deployment and before D.J.'s birth; a narrow window of opportunity.

In the end, Colt did not qualify for speech services through the school for the first set of tests but I hoped the tubes would clear up his ears, thus helping his speech to improve on its own.

Colt's speech did improve after the surgery, but he continued to mispronounce words. A second evaluation, performed by school personnel, qualified him for services and he received sixty minutes of speech therapy per week. In the fall, he also attended the Title I Preschool, which aided in his speech improvements. I had worried about him attending because all preschoolers had to be toilet trained and he was not fully there yet. Thankfully, he figured it out just in time.

Once he developed a routine with preschool and started talking better, Colt became as sweet as ever. I drove him to therapy once a week for his thirty-minute sessions. I felt guilty for ignoring him at home, though. D.J., who had been born by then, required most of my attention.

Yes, D.J. was learning to scoot around, clap his hands and pull up on furniture to stand. He even survived his first haircut. (No more hippy child!) However, he refused to hold his bottle, and he experienced problems with his bowels. He had one bout of diarrhea that lasted three weeks. The doctor changed his formula again. Not only that, he would frequently wake up at night. Eventually, he developed bronchitis, which meant breathing treatments. I was exhausted, and at times I resented Hunter and D.J. They were ruining my chances of getting sleep and experiencing peace in the house.

Of course, God is good and full of surprises. He healed D.J.'s eye after our pastor prayed for him at his dedication ceremony. His tear duct opened and the mucus had cleared up. He was four months of age and because the tear duct opened, the need for surgery disappeared.

As I reflected on God's small miracle for my youngest son, I constantly wondered how parents survived raising kids without having faith, which had carried me through the motherhood journey thus far. One of my journal entries said,

"Everyone is doing well. D.J. is sitting up, trying to crawl, and eating baby food. Hunter is learning to write words and read. Colt is cleaning up, talking better, and helping me at home. Yes, I have good boys. Gotta love them!"

In following year of 2010, some more positive events brought a smile to face and made me love my boys all the more. When spring arrived, we spent time outdoors. Hunter and Colt rode their bikes, played in the sand, and rode their Power Wheels four wheeler. They also rode on the mower with Danny as he cut the grass.

Later on in the month of April, D.J. turned the BIG ONE. Most of the family attended the party. D.J. liked his gifts and made a mess with his transportation cake. He ate his first McDonald's Happy Meal, too. He walked shortly after his first birthday, and he appeared to be on schedule at his well child check-up. The only concern noted by the pediatrician was the absence of words. D.J. was not talking yet. We hoped it was just that he was a late talker.

No matter what happened, I reminded myself to focus on God and the good aspects of my life. My kids were my joy even if they tested my patience. The resentment I held toward Hunter and D.J. at times did not affect my love for them or the pride I had in their accomplishments. Hunter received seven awards at the school's end of year assembly, and Colt completed preschool with satisfactory marks.

Throughout the summer the boys enjoyed the usual child-hood delights like going on rides at the fair, catching candy being thrown from the parade floats, barbecuing with Daddy, visiting family, and racing through the yard. We gazed in wonder at fireworks on the Fourth of July. Colt covered his ears and cried while Hunter laughed and D.J. slept.

Maybe I should set off fireworks all night and D.J. would sleep!

On July 15th that year, it was Colt's turn to be five-years-old. We let him spend the day at the Magic House. Later on, several members of our family came to our house and watched him open his presents and eat his race car cake. He played with his new monster trucks, race cars, play dough, and bubble gun.

The only summer mishap was that Hunter developed an ear infection.

Oh no. Does this mean more antibiotics and doctor appointments?

No. This infection was an isolated incident thankfully. His ear cleared up and he did not need new tubes. His old tubes had fallen out and he was on the road to normal hearing and normal ear function.

Overall, the boys were doing well. In the fall of 2010, Hunter and Colt started the school year at their new school. Both boys excelled in their work. As we had expected, Hunter proved to be more advanced than other same age peers. He was no longer in the gifted program, though, as the district no longer had the funds to operate the program.

I felt a little sad as I completed Colt's baby book, and when I dropped him off in the gym that first day for kindergarten. I missed both of the older boys during the day. The house was quiet.

The only noise I heard was D.J. crying and gesturing for his needs. Since he was nonverbal, these were the means in which he used to communicate. I kept hoping he would talk on his own. Was he truly a late talker?

He also had patches of bumpy skin, but we finally did get an answer to explain that.

"He has Keratosis Pilaris," the dermatologist said.

"Finally, an explanation for the bumps on his arms and legs. Not eczema as everyone suggested," I told the doctor.

"It's genetic too." She informed me.

"Oh. That explains the bumps on my arms and legs then. I thought they were acne. Now I know." I rubbed my arms, looking at the bumps.

"I will say this, the skin condition doesn't affect your health, but it is annoying. Some days are worse than others. Diet doesn't play a role either. The only suggestion I have is to use the CeraVe cream. I have found that it works pretty well. You can find it in stores such as Wal-Mart," she informed me. I thanked her and added a Wal-Mart trip to my to-do list.

In no time, the fall events and holidays came. For Halloween, the kids trick-or-treated in the cool, night air. Hunter chose to be the Transformer Bumblebee, Colt dressed as a fireman, and we dressed D.J. up like a monkey. It was quite the sight watching those three go door-to-door asking for candy!

We celebrated Thanksgiving and Christmas with our extended families as we had every year. We put up the tree and shopped for Christmas. The boys visited Santa, which was fun despite poor D.J. crying at the white-bearded man.

I saved him from the strange looking fellow. "What's wrong D.J.? It's okay. He's Santa and he brings you presents. He's really nice."

D.J. stopped crying. He sucked on the middle fingers of his left hand and with his big brown eyes, observed the guy in the red suit. It really seemed that he understood what I said. If only he could *tell* me what he needed. Any words he had said were no longer there. He waved bye-bye one day and stopped the next day. He never held his bottle. I couldn't figure out what was going on with my Little Man.

He reached other milestones on time and he had the cutest smile that melted the hearts of those around him. All the boys had sweet smiles. I looked at Hunter and Colt still sitting on Santa's lap. They were chattering away.

"…I want a monstew twuck," Colt said.

All the boys had changed so much the past year and a half as had I. I allowed God to show me how to love as He does, especially with my children. With Christmas upon us, the celebration of Jesus brought to mind the love He had for children.

Instead of focusing on the boys' faults, I began to see them as God did. All the new milestones and fun times brought out their true value for me. They were gifts that grew (literally!) better with time. I had to show them love as Jesus did and not let my response to negative feelings or actions prevent them from seeing His love in me.

At the end of 2010, Hunter and Colt participated in a Christmas program at school and Kathy attended the show as part of a special Grandparent's Day. The boys sang with the group and made us proud! For Christmas break, the family opened presents while looking at the snow outside. We had a white Christmas that year. Perfect! The pure white of the snow symbolized the purity of His love that I wanted.

"Dear Father,

Thank You for showing me a newfound love for my boys, despite their imperfections. They are blessings. Your love for me is what has let me love them, even D.J. and Hunter who caused feelings of resentment in me. Forgive me for relying on myself to love them. True and unconditional love comes from You. If I don't have Your love, then I can't fully love them. I can't expect them to be perfect if I am not either. They are still so young! I want to lead them to You, and I can't do that if I'm not living as an example of Christ. Continue to reveal ways to love them even when I don't know how. In Jesus' name. Amen."

CHAPTER SEVENTEEN

BLESSINGS IN THE MIDST OF CHAOS

"Sons are a heritage from the LORD, children a reward from him. Like arrows in the hands of a warrior are sons born in one's youth. Blessed is the man whose quiver is full of them. They will not be put to shame when they contend with their enemies in the gate."
Psalm 127:3-5

"Oh man! There's blood in my urine!" I called out. I contacted my urologist, who ordered a CT Scan.

"You have three kidney stones," The nurse told me. "You have one large stone and one small stone in your right kidney and one small stone in your left kidney."

"That's not as bad as the eight I had the first time, but they hurt anyway."

This time all three stones were treated at once with the lithotripsy procedure. I almost felt relief until my blood pressure shot up to 160/110. The doctors and nurses kept walking into my hospital room with concerned looks on their faces, causing me to panic even more. The last news I wanted to hear was that I would need blood pressure medication, or worse yet, that I was having a heart attack. I had enough to do with raising three kids, balancing our finances, and taking on all the household responsibilities.

Come on Lord. Lower my blood pressure. I can't do this right now. I have too much to do.

By His grace and after resting three to four extra hours, my blood pressure lowered enough for me to go home.

Thank you Lord. I've said this before, but You always come through for me.

I recovered quickly and then within a few months later, I anticipated another procedure. My kidney stones weren't the only health issue. My gallbladder, which still had a stone, caused me to feel sick. It had to come out as soon as possible. The best day available for the procedure was that Good Friday, in 2010.

"Why did you choose Good Friday?" people kept asking me.

"I don't want to cancel D.J.'s first birthday or be sick anymore," I had answered repeatedly. "Sorry, no Easter at our house this year."

The surgery was a success, but once at home my patience was tested. Toys scattered the floor, dirty dishes filled the sink, and clothes piled up in the bathroom. While I gave Danny credit for taking care of the boys, I needed to rest. I couldn't sleep with having to get up and down to constantly answer questions or show Danny what to do.

Not only that, against my wishes, our families visited us for Easter. I appreciated them wanting to see us but at the same time, I was tired and sore from the procedure. Kathy, sensing my frustration, offered to keep D.J. overnight. She was such a blessing, always there when I needed her, even if she wasn't feeling well or had other plans.

As I said before, we celebrated my "Little Man's" first birthday and like his big brothers, he devoured his chocolate cake. Mother's Day was next, and I purchased a Busy Mom's Bible for myself. I enjoyed visiting with my mom and Kathy, especially with the exciting news I was keeping inside. I was expecting Baby #4!! This pregnancy caught me off guard. Did the antibiotics used during my surgery weaken my birth control, or was it losing effectiveness, or both?

In the end, however, it didn't matter how it happened. There was no doubt that I carried a child. The pink lines showed up within a matter of seconds on both pregnancy tests. Our next Hunka Hunka Burnin' Love was due January 8, 2011 (I'm sure you know, but that is Elvis Presley's birthday).

It was the Friday of Mother's Day weekend, and the boys had gone to bed already. Danny and I were stunned. I vividly remember both of us sitting on the couch, speechless. We were definitely excited, but also totally overwhelmed.

"I can't believe we will have four kids!" I finally exclaimed. "What are we going to do?"

"We need a bigger house," Danny sighed.

"So we need to get this one ready to sell and contact our real estate agent then?"

"Yeah, I will call him Monday."

After seeing my OB/GYN, I prayed, "Lord, I don't know if I can do this. Especially since the doctor asked me to quit taking my Paxil for the first trimester. I used it for the entirety of my last three pregnancies, but I realize there's a risk to the baby's health. Please keep me and the baby healthy through this. Calm my nerves."

In addition, I wrote this in my journal at the end of May as a way to encourage myself:

"Just stop and smell the roses once and awhile. Keep my focus on God. I definitely need His strength."

I realized I would have a first grader, a kindergartener, a toddler, and a baby soon. My confidence in my ability to care for four children was shaky at best. One, two, or three kids I could handle, but four? I had to brush away the comments from people with only one child or no children at all who said, 'Can you handle four kids?' or 'When is Baby #5 coming?' They may not have meant to sound judgemental, or maybe they just didn't understand how their words affected me.

Most people, though, were happy for us. Both Danny and I looked forward to meeting our newest member of the family, boy or girl. A part of me wanted a boy since I had three already and thought I knew what to expect there. However, a girl would bring some variety. Universally, our family hoped for a girl. Danny and I agreed on the name Autumn Elizabeth for a girl and the name Levi Alexander for a boy. We wanted to be prepared when we found out the gender that August, which for me, couldn't come soon enough.

Summer came. Danny left for two weeks of training with the Army National Guard, and I stayed busy with the kids. We visited our in-laws, checked out books from the library, and played for hours outside. Kathy watched the boys so I could shop and get some much needed "me" time.

Danny returned home Father's Day weekend and the kids and I spent all our time with him. We waited until the following weekend to visit my dad. He understood why we didn't come sooner.

Despite all the chaos, I cared for myself the best ways possible. I had regular adjustments from the chiropractor for my back and hips, and my annual eye exam. At my regular OB/GYN appointment, I brought up the problem of a growing hernia at my gallbladder incision site by my belly button.

"It's the size of a golf ball," I said, showing it to him.

"Just wait on fixing it until after the baby is born. The surgery is too risky while pregnant unless it becomes life threatening," he replied. True, but patience was still not a virtue I possessed to any great degree.

When I started my second trimester, the doctor allowed me to take my Paxil again. I also tried hard to "give it all" to God. I was still struggling with that. I had a tendency to fall away from Him in times of stress. What a difference I felt when I did give it up to His capable hands! I felt better emotionally and did not feel alone or unhappy.

Danny and I had reached good terms again after some minor squabbling we had been doing. We could not stay angry with each other for long, especially when we received exciting news about the gender of our baby. After two attempts, the ultrasound technician told us we were having a baby girl! I had wondered if the baby was a girl since she was being so modest about revealing herself.

"Are you sure it's a girl?" I asked, trying to sit up so I could see the picture better.

"I am ninety-nine percent sure," she answered, pointing out the female characteristics of the baby on the screen.

"So Danny, what do you have to say now? You are not too manly to have a girl are you?" I retorted.

"No," he answered sheepishly, staring at the ultrasound machine.

Danny did not comment about the baby right away. He was obviously taken aback about the news, which I didn't understand.

"How will I take care of a girl?" he asked, eyes wide with worry.

"The same way you take care of the boys. You will know what to do," everyone assured him. Though still unsure, he accepted the reality of having a girl, and we all continued to let him know we believed he would be a great dad to her.

I began buying pink and purple items immediately. I called and texted our family and friends as fast as I could type in the numbers and the words. Everyone was thrilled to hear the news that they would have a niece or granddaughter soon and Hunter, Colt, and D.J. would have a little sister.

That fall, my sister-in-law, Julie hosted a baby shower for me. My wonderful family and friends gave generously and supplied most of our needs; bottles, a diaper bag, baby girl clothes, crib sheets, bumper pads, and several packs of diapers, all for my Autumn Elizabeth. I was almost ready for her.

We almost had a house too. A contract had been signed on our current home, and then we had signed a contract on an earth home. It had been built in 2002 on eighteen acres of land. When the buyers for our house changed their minds, we had to terminate the other contract. Disappointing, to say the least.

I focused instead on what my gut had been telling me all along. I had been worried about the new home's distant location and the lack of windows in the bedrooms, an easy escape route in case of a fire. In rainy times the nearby creek would flood and I would be housebound until it receded again. I believed God protected us from possible disaster.

I put my faith in Him to help us find the right home when we decided to look again. Deciding to wait on His timing, we took our house off the market before the holidays began.

At this point in time, we needed to concentrate on our growing family, especially with our soon-to-be new arrival. All the bags were packed. With my pregnancy term dragging on and on, I was getting more and more impatient, I did not want a big belly anymore, and I wanted to meet Autumn. What did she look like? Would she sleep and eat well? Most importantly, would she be healthy?

"Dear Father,

Life can sure be chaotic. I hope 2011 will bring more blessings. Time will tell. Whatever happens, You are there for us every step of the way. I have nothing to fear. Maybe we will have a new home.

I am eager to meet Autumn. I faced many struggles this past year, but despite them all, You brought her as a gift for us. I cannot thank You enough! Forgive me for not recognizing that You were with me in the midst of the surgeries, with my unexpected pregnancy, and in the search for a new home. I still need to trust You and seek You for complete peace. Help me keep recognizing Your presence in every circumstance. In Jesus' name. Amen."

CHAPTER EIGHTEEN

KEEPING A STRONG MARRIAGE

≈

"Be completely humble and gentle; be patient, bearing
with one another in love. Make every effort to keep
the unity of the Spirit through the bond of peace."
Ephesians 4:2-3

"Above all, love each other deeply, because love covers
over a multitude of sins." 1 Peter 4:8

Life had been a whirlwind of stressful events and the stability of Danny's and my relationship had been challenged along the troublesome path.

"You have no right to be upset about the dispatching job slowing down," Danny said to me. He sat at the computer typing a home inspection report. I stood in the doorway of the office. The boys ran about the house.

"You aren't upset? Don't you want the money?" I asked, wondering why I was the only one feeling so stressed.

"Of course I want the income, but I'm doing home inspections and I'm doing well right now."

"I know. But then there's the weather and school being closed. The boys have been home more."

"So? That's life. Get over it. You have it pretty good. You have no right to complain," Danny replied.

Oh man. Lord, what he doesn't understand is that I desperately need a break. I haven't told him because I hoped he'd figure it out. These feelings of bitterness and unhappiness are taking their toll on me. I can't blame the kids for not knowing how to help me. Danny, on the other hand, has quit showing compassion. What happened? Before he deployed to Kosovo, he would never have been so cold-hearted.

I felt Danny and I simply needed more time together to reconnect as husband and wife again. We did celebrate Valentine's Day together though. We ate at Stefanina's and watched <u>Avatar</u>. Despite that, I still felt as if our relationship was dying like the flowers Danny had given me. A quiet desperate part deep inside of me just wanted to quit trying at all. When Alan proposed to his girlfriend on Valentine's Day, I almost told him to not take that step.

Marriage is a hard job and to keep one healthy requires that both people be fully committed to each other and to God. As a couple grows closer to God, they grow closer to each other. This is the threefold cord I'd heard taught from the pulpit so many times

As for Danny and me, I am certain our relationship would have seen improvement if we had prayed together more. I was completing daily devotionals, if nothing else, but spiritually we weren't connecting very often. Attending church regularly was challenging because of winter weather, sick kids, and my mostly absentee husband. The few times I did make it to church, I stayed in the nursery to help. I barely had a chance to sit in the adult service to hear God's word preached. My Heavenly Father seemed to be distant. I needed to feel Him close and to feel his comfort. I felt alone.

Thankfully, Lareesa never left my side, figuratively speaking. She lived one thousand miles away, but she talked to me often and at any time, day or night. She also encouraged me to join Facebook.

Now here was some hope. Even If I could not connect with my husband, I could stay in touch with old friends and acquaintances.

If only my computer's settings had been compatible, or I knew how to change them to make the internet connection happen.

Maybe another time down the road.

I had to believe I'd find the friends I needed to connect with on a deeper level. Most of my current friends were more like acquaintances.

That evening, after my Facebook failure, I watched the boys playing in the living room. Hunter opened and closed his WALL-E toy. Colt and D.J. built with Duplo blocks. Danny rested, listening intently to a show on the History Channel. He deserved to relax, but I'd been working hard, too. By this time I was pregnant with Autumn, and I became tired faster. I needed his help. I didn't feel good and I still had to clean the kitchen, bathe the boys, and put them to bed.

"Danny, I know you're worn out too, but I feel like I'm last on your list. When I do ask for help, you don't do it, even after agreeing. You're always available to help other people, just not me. Why?" I wrung the dish cloth in my hands.

"I don't put you last," he said, slapping the remote down and glaring at me. "I help you more than other husbands. I'm always here when I'm not working."

"Then would you reschedule the home inspection you have tomorrow? I'm sick. I think it's morning sickness."

"I can't. The client needs it done. I'll call Mom."

"That's fine but I'd rather have you here. Don't you care?"

"Come on Lisa. You know I love you, but I have to do this. You want to stay home, don't you?"

"Yeah," I answered. I was not sure he meant it when he said he loved me.

The boys didn't say a word or make a sound. They didn't comprehend the issues their Mommy and Daddy were having. For them, they were absorbed in their own worlds and probably thought the fighting was normal. I knew it wasn't. Not that much.

I retreated to our bedroom and stretched out on the bed. I cried out to God.

"Lord! Something has to give here. I don't know what to do. I can't ask anyone to pray for Danny and me. Then they would know we were having problems. How embarrassing! People look up to us and think we have the perfect marriage. What would they say? I don't want to hear the typical comments such as 'Have you seen a counselor?' or 'Maybe you are overreacting.' or 'Give it some time.' I have given it time and it's only getting worse. I don't want to divorce Danny but I can't live like this. Neither can I ask the boys or Autumn to live like this."

"Lisa, you need to communicate with Danny better. You can't expect him to know how you feel or to be perfect. Be patient with him. Be thankful for what you have and ask for help more than you do now. Don't you want a strong marriage for the kids? Don't you want to be a role model of love for them? Then love Danny even when you think he doesn't deserve it. I have loved you at your worst. Do the same for Danny. Love him as you love the boys," God quietly spoke to me.

For our tenth anniversary, Danny and I ate at the Stonehill Restaurant and walked on the riverfront in Hermann, Missouri. During another outing, the boys stayed with family overnight while Danny and I enjoyed a dinner cruise in Hannibal, Missouri.

"How nice to have no kids for a night! We don't see each other that much. We need these dates to remember the reasons we married in the beginning and to rekindle our love.

Lately, we have fought more than I like. We need to smile together more. Have more fun," I told Danny as we stood on the deck of the boat.

"Yes. I'm sorry I've been hard on you. I didn't mean to make you feel bad. I just want you to be happy. Are you happy?" he asked, his eyes looking hopeful.

"Of course I am! At least I am now. I admit I was not happy when you were acting ugly. The deployment must have thrown you off for some reason."

"I guess. I don't know what happened. I think it's the stress of having to provide for the family."

"I could see that. Sorry if I haven't supported you enough. I'll do better."

"I know…I love you."

"I love you, too." This time I knew he meant it when he said he loved me.

During the following months, Danny and I truly reconnected. I had shared my feelings with him and he apologized. We smiled more and fought less.

When we celebrated my birthday, Danny surprised me during dinner by giving me a sparkling heart pendant.

"Oh, Danny! It's beautiful. You must love me to give me this." My face glowed with pure joy.

"I have always loved you, even if I don't always show it." He reached over the table to hold my hand.

Through his gaze, I could see the love in his eyes, and I squeezed his hand. We both smiled. I knew then we would be okay. We had many blessings to enjoy, including the upcoming birth of our precious daughter Autumn. She was on her way.

"Dear Father,

Thank You for showing me that I need to love Danny even when he may not show his love for me. I'm sorry for being selfish and complaining about my life. I need to communicate with Danny more about how I feel. I can't expect him to figure me out. I want to ask that You help us find time to pray together more. We have to keep a strong marriage so our kids can have the best lives possible. I want to see love, joy, and peace reign in our home. In Jesus' name. Amen."

CHAPTER NINETEEN

HARD WORK PAYS OFF

~

"He who works his land will have abundant food, but he who chases fantasies lacks judgment." Proverbs 12:11

"The sluggard craves and gets nothing, but the desires of the diligent are fully satisfied." Proverbs 13:4

Autumn was on her way and my marriage was on the mend. However, we still had to address the continuing issues of finances and our house.

"So you will do the load for that price?" I asked the broker on the phone. "That's great! Thank you!" I said as I hung up the phone.

"YES!" I shouted as I dialed Alan's number and jumped out of the chair. "Hey Alan. I got that load you wanted going out west and guess what? They agreed to do it at the rate you wanted."

"That's great sis! Thank you!"

"You're welcome."

Another good paying load to add to the books. I've been finding a lot of those lately. I have to give God the credit. He's the one showing me where to find them. Not only will Alan get the money he needs, I'll get ten percent. I'm so relieved! Now we can pay off some of those bills we have.

Later that day, I shared my encouraging news with Danny as he cooked dinner. I stood next to him as he stirred the pasta and I could smell the spaghetti sauce simmering on the stove.

"Hey Danny. Guess what? I found a good paying load for Alan. Another one. Now we can pay on some of the bills. The load is going out west, which means more miles which means more money!."

"That's good. When does he head out?"

"Tomorrow."

"I have good news too."

"Oh yeah. Did you get another home inspection?"

"Yep. For tomorrow."

"That makes four this month, right? We need to celebrate!!"

"Not so fast."

"Uh oh. What?" I asked reluctantly.

"The buyers on the house decided to terminate the contract." (Yes, this is about us losing the home we had wanted and the same one I had mentioned earlier).

"Because of the basement?"

"They weren't comfortable with the leaks or the cracks in its walls."

159

"We have to terminate the contract on that earth home, don't we? That sucks. I really liked that house. Does God not want us to have a bigger house? Was I wrong about moving five years ago? Are we going to be stuck in this little house? I give up," I said, sitting down. "We will just have to add on somehow. If God isn't going to help us we have no choice. Why did I trust Him? It's not fair." My pity party was in full swing. I didn't handle disappointment well.

"He will help us find another house. Do you want to take our house off the market until we fix the basement?"

"Why not? We aren't going to sell the house unless we do that. No one wants a leaky basement. I know I was leery about the windows and the creek but I liked that other house," I flinched at my whiny voice.

"I know. I did too. But maybe it'll be there after we fix the basement. I can call Robin and ask him how much it would be to reinforce the walls and seal up the cracks."

"All right. Whatever. I don't care. Even if we fix it, who says we are going to sell it? Who says we would still get the other house? Why would we have anything good like that happen to us? God doesn't care. He's probably on His throne laughing at us right now. Like, 'Ha ha, they didn't sell their house. I'm going to make them stay where they are.'" Not only was my pity party in full swing, but the band was just getting warmed up.

"No He isn't. You know that isn't true. We'll find a house when it's the right time. Don't give up."

"I sure want to. All that hoping for nothing."

While our house's foundation was solid, no one wanted to buy the home with a problematic basement. So, after losing the deal, we took it off the market. With Danny's cousin, Robin, in charge of the project, the walls and the ceiling were reinforced. Danny's brothers and my brothers offered their assistance, too. They used a skid loader and shovels to dig the dirt away from the outside of the house and a jackhammer to pound away the concrete floor of the basement for the beams. Once they were in place, the men poured new concrete around the beams and then refilled the outside hole with dirt. While the men repaired our house, the kids and I visited family for the day. I didn't need the boys getting in the way or getting hurt.

While this type of job would normally cost thousands of dollars, with our families' help, the only expenses we had were renting the skid loader, buying the concrete and paying Robin for his expertise and time.

Danny fed all the men a delicious meal of grilled steaks. No one complained about the food or about sacrificing their time and effort to help us. Although the men had completed the hard labor with no pay really, they remained cheerful and upbeat. As they worked, they joked and laughed, at least while I was there. Besides the floor, wall and ceiling work, Danny also replaced the steps in the basement. The bottom ones had rotted from previous flooding. We hoped the new improvements would increase the chances of the house selling.

Witnessing the selfless attitude of my family during that all day project, I cringed inside. I was ashamed at myself for being so ungrateful about so many things. I shouldn't have griped about losing the new house or not selling our current home. I knew deep down that God's hand had guided the events. Being thankful in all circumstances and working hard paid off if I practiced patience until the answer came. I was slowly learning the lessons God was teaching.

I had to appreciate the good aspects of my life, such as the success of Danny's business and my dispatching job. My focus shouldn't be on the negative, or what I perceived as negative. Losing a contract on the other house could be seen as a blessing. The door had opened for us to find a home better suited to our needs and desires. My response should've been prayer, not complaining. Not only did I have to work hard physically to help us find a new home and sell our old one, I had to work hard spiritually by seeking out what God would have us to do. He cared, and He showed it, if I would just look with grateful eyes. I had to do my part too. God wasn't just going make everything better all of the sudden. Blessings came with following God's will, not my own.

"Dear Father,

Thank You that our basement is fixed. Not only are the walls reinforced, the steps are fixed too. I know we'll find a buyer for our house and we'll find a house for us. I have to trust You on this. I know you will reward us because we worked hard. For those You have chosen to do Your will, You bless abundantly, but only after they do their part too. You don't just suddenly make life easier. Our life has definitely not been easy this year. We are still on a tight budget. However, the home inspection business is prospering and I'm finding good paying loads for Alan now. I couldn't be happier. Forgive me for complaining, once again, about the problems we have. Help me praise You even when life is hard. In Jesus' name. Amen."

CHAPTER TWENTY

DAYS OF BLESSING WITH MY CHILDREN

"This is the day the LORD has made; let us rejoice and be glad in it." Psalm 118:24

"O uch!"

I woke up with pressure and contractions. Were they Braxton-Hicks contractions or real ones? I was only three days from my due date but I wasn't sure. I didn't want to bother Danny for a false alarm. I didn't want a repeat of what happened with Colt.

My phone rang.

Oh good. That's Danny. Saves me from having to decide to call him or not! Instead, Alan's name appeared on the screen, not Danny's. *Oh no. I wonder what he wants.*

"Hello?" I answered. I stood at the kitchen counter watching D.J. playing with his toy car on the floor. Hunter and Colt were at school.

"Hey, uh, Lisa? Can I bring up these load sheets tonight for you to invoice?"

"I won't be home. I have a doctor appointment...and I think I'm in labor," I said.

"Oh really?"

"No kidding. I'm having contractions five minutes apart. I haven't told Danny yet because I didn't want him to worry in case it's a false alarm. He's finishing up a home inspection right now but I'm going to call him soon. He should be almost done." I said, wincing from pain. Another contraction.

"Will you be okay?" Alan asked with concern in his voice.

"I'm fine. Don't worry. And sorry about the invoices. I can do them in a few days," I assured him.

"Oh, don't worry about that. You take care of yourself. Take as much time as you need."

He actually said to take as much time as I need. That's a first. I guess he's realizing how difficult this is for me.

Lareesa also called me and I told her the news. "You sure you'll be okay, sis?" she asked.

"Yes. I am sure. Don't worry. I will call Danny soon. I want him to finish his home inspection."

About one o'clock that afternoon I called Danny. I could wait no longer.

As soon as Danny's voice was heard on the other end I blurted out, "Danny, I think I'm in labor! Are you almost done?"

"Uh yeah, I can stop and finish this later. I told the buyers you were close to having the baby and they understood if I had to leave early. I'll be home soon. Are you okay?"

"Yeah, but what about the boys? Should we pick them up from school and head to your mom's?"

"It wouldn't hurt."

I loaded up the bags while Danny called the school. He explained the situation with the secretary. Even though it was past two o'clock, she broke the normal dismissal protocol and changed the boys' pick up status to car rider.

My contractions slowed down on the way to Kathy's so we decided to wait until that evening for my regularly scheduled appointment. For two hours, I sat at the table in Kathy's dining room, smelling vegetable soup warming in the crockpot, and glancing every few minutes at the clock.

At dinner time, I gulped down the soup, kissed the boys goodbye, and gave Kathy last minute instructions on their bedtime routine. Danny and I didn't say much in the van.

Is this really happening? What will the doctor say? I really hope he says I'm in labor.

Once we arrived and the doctor examined me, he said, "You are three to four centimeters dilated. Your body is certainly getting ready for the big show! With your history of short labor, and considering you live forty-five minutes from the hospital, I think it's best to admit you tonight. I will tell the staff you'll be induced in the morning if you do not go on your own tonight. Is that okay with you?"

"Oh yes. That's fine! I am ready, for sure!"

"And *please* have the nurses call me if you go into active labor during the night," he requested.

"Okay. I will," I promised.

I was just as excited to see my fourth baby born as I was with my first. The only difference: experience. Without a doubt, I knew I would have Autumn before the night was over. The doctor would have to be called. The nurse, on the other hand, did not take me seriously.

"I'm having more pain. Should you hook me up to the monitors again?" I asked. She had removed them to allow me free movement.

"You'll be fine. I can give you something for the pain if you want. Just try to relax."

Lady, I know my body and what's going on here! I don't need a Tylenol. And I can't relax like this!

About an hour later the head nurse came in. My contractions were stronger and closer together. "You're five centimeters dilated. You are going to have this baby tonight. I'll call the doctor."

I looked over at that know-it-all nurse. *See! I AM in labor. This is baby number four so I know my body!*

The head nurse then asked, "Do you want an epidural?"

"Yes, please!"

The medicine worked so well that I fell asleep around midnight. The nurse woke me up around two in the morning and checked me. I was fully dilated. I had slept through labor! That was a first.

Was this a sign? Would this recovery be easy?

"Time for you to have this baby!" The nurse said.

My doctor came in. I didn't push for long. At 2:35 a.m., January 6, 2011, Autumn Elizabeth was born. I finally had a daughter and she was beautiful. She resembled Colt as a newborn with the chubby cheeks and generous amount of dark hair. She proved to be my heaviest baby weighing 8 pounds, 9 ounces! She was 21 inches long, healthy and such a sleeper! I had to wake her for feedings.

After resting for three days in the hospital, I was ready to go home to be with Danny and the boys. The only times I had seen them was during their brief evening visits to see Autumn. I received visits from other family, too. I had to laugh when the nurse asked if Mike was the grandpa!

Once home, I had to straighten up the house and settle in with Autumn. Alan said I could take a few days off. I appreciated his kindness. I rested and recovered while getting acquainted with my baby girl. Two sweet ladies from church brought meals for us, as well. One of the ladies, Tina, would later play a vital role in my spiritual growth and in the making of this book.

Colt and D.J. adored their new sister, but Hunter seemed to be very angry about the new addition. He hit and talked back. He broke the front of our dishwasher, put a hole in our card table, and broke one of my belts. Was he feeling ignored, displaced, or just developing cabin fever?

It snowed a full eighteen inches from a blizzard on Hunter's birthday. That storm caused the Midwest to shut down. Snowdrifts reached four feet in our area. Danny tried to clear our driveway with the shovel but his back was hurting him. Our neighbor offered to clear it with his tractor and Danny could not have been more thankful.

"This snow day is a gift from the weather," I told Hunter, trying to cheer him up.

"Yeah. I can play with my new toys and in the snow!" he said, his face beaming.

Missouri sure had crazy weather! One year it was a tornado, and then another year a blizzard, for Hunter's special day. Since we knew the storm was coming we celebrated his special day early. We never knew what to expect.

Standing by the kitchen window and holding Autumn, I watched the boys slide down the big mounds of snow.

Might as well enjoy the snow somehow.

With the fresh air and extra attention from his birthday, Hunter's emotions calmed.

Thank you Lord, I silently prayed.

Colt and D.J. stared at Autumn with curiosity. D.J. didn't utter a word but Colt shared his feelings.

"I love Autumn," Colt said with admiration. He bonded with his sister because we told him she looked like him as a baby.

His speech had progressed enough that even people outside the family understood him more.

On the other hand, people still questioned if D.J. had autism because he didn't talk. I had taught kids with autism, and I knew D.J. didn't have the disorder. He matched colors and shapes, built complex block structures, and made eye contact. I knew he was smart and understood what others said. I didn't know why he lacked expressive language, but I believed he was not only a late developer in that area but also in the area of toilet training. Some days I felt as if I would be changing diapers and pull-ups forever!

However, as frustrated as I felt in raising the kids, life was short and I did not want to miss opportunities to spend time with them. I had feared for our safety due to severe weather outbreaks that late spring.

One afternoon, about mid-May, D.J. and Autumn napped peacefully in their beds about the time that Hunter and Colt were scheduled to come home from school. The sky darkened and clouds threatened to unleash a raging storm. I tried to call Danny and there was no answer, which I later found out was because he had been ordered to hunker down in a vault. Tornado warnings flashed across the television with maps showing possible locations of twisters. One was near Danny and in no time, that same storm traveled my direction. The electricity flickered off.

I peeked in on D.J. and Autumn, wondering if I should take them into the hall. (The new steps had not yet been replaced in the basement so the only way down was by ladder. Not an option with two sleepy toddlers.) An eerie silence covered the house. I glanced out the living room window.

"What the heck?" I shouted, not believing my own eyes. A small tornado, about two miles north, bounced along the horizon. I grabbed my two little ones and raced to the hallway. I sat D.J. down and sat huddled, still holding Autumn. Knock! Knock! Knock! Was that my racing heart or someone at the door?

I peered around the corner. A strange lady stood at the door. Not wanting her out in the storm I opened the door. "Please come in! Hurry!" I said.

"Thank you for letting me in. I saw the tornado and wanted to get to shelter. I'm coming back from a doctor appointment."

"We can all wait in the hall. I have my two little ones with me. We'll be safe there."

The lady introduced herself and looked outside. The twister had disappeared. We both breathed a sigh of relief. That was too close for comfort. The school called about a late dismissal and the bus driver called too. He had to use a different route because of debris on the roads. When the boys climbed off the bus, I hugged them tight. They were safe. We were all safe, including Danny, who arrived home shortly after the boys.

The lady who stopped at my house that day sent me a thank you card. The storm was rated an F1, causing only minor damage to buildings and downed power lines.

With that scare over and a renewed appreciation for life, I treasured the time spent with the boys and Autumn. We enjoyed

Hunter's and Colt's T-Ball practices and games. Being a lefty, Hunter was asked to pitch for his team. When at bat, he smacked that ball hard and when in the field, he willingly chased after the balls. Unsure of what to do when in the field, Colt drifted into dreamland on occasion, but he smacked the ball at his turn to bat. The boys' grins from the dugout warmed my heart. In the bleachers, D.J. and Autumn giggled at one another's silly antics and munched on their snacks.

How precious you kids are to me!

Toward the end of summer, Danny enrolled in fiddle lessons. Hunter followed suit. He had seen the remake of the movie Karate Kid and liked the part where the young girl skillfully played the violin. He liked the karate parts too but I told him he needed to pick one activity. Cub Scouts and fiddle lessons were enough. The same applied to Colt, who decided to take guitar lessons.

Colt tired of the guitar two months later, but Hunter kept playing his fiddle. His talent showed when he played "Frosty the Snowman" during the school's Christmas program. He showed no signs of nervousness. A natural! I wished Danny had seen the performance, but he was training out of town. Our new babysitter stayed with Autumn and D.J. (I liked her. She was a keeper.)

For the holidays, the kids and I put up the Christmas tree the day after Thanksgiving per request of Danny, who always says, "Let Thanksgiving have its day."

172

Danny and I let the kids visit Santa. D.J. was still uncertain of the jolly old man, but the other three kids eagerly sat on his lap. The older boys named off the items on their lists, placing their confidence in their good behavior that year. Why wouldn't they receive all they wanted?

Autumn was almost one and walking. Her eyes widened with excitement at the lights and at the mountain of toys under the tree on Christmas morning. What was all this commotion about? Her brothers ripped open their presents as she tried to tear the paper off hers with help from mommy. All the kids' eyes glistened. Their wishes had come true, and so had mine. Nothing was better than spending time with my family, all six of us.

Our family was complete in the sense that Danny and I had decided we didn't want any more kids. I loved them dearly but four was enough. We needed time to find ourselves in Christ; To be complete in Him.

"Dear Father,

Thank You for the time you give me with the kids. Thank You for Autumn. She has brought fulfillment to our family. May I rejoice in the days with my children, good or bad. Forgive me for not appreciating them enough. They are blessings, not burdens. Thank You for keeping us safe during the storms too. I trust You with our lives. It is through You that we are truly complete. In Jesus' name. Amen."

CHAPTER TWENTY-ONE

HELP IN TIME OF NEED

"O LORD my God, I called to you for help and you healed me. O LORD, you brought me up from the grave; you spared me from going down into the pit."
Psalm 30:2-3

"Two are better than one, because they have a good return for their work: If one falls down, his friend can help him up. But pity the man who falls and had no one to help him up! Also, if two lie down together, they will keep warm. But how can one keep warm alone? Though one may be overpowered, two can defend themselves. A cord of three strands is not quickly broken."
Ecclesiastes 4:9-12

"What are we going to do about a babysitter? No one is available and I'm worried I won't be able to keep up with the kids after my hernia surgery. It's so frustrating! I wish people kept their word when they offered to watch the kids," I lamented to Danny, feeding Autumn some of her baby food. "My hernia surgery is coming up and it'd be nice if I had someone here to help with the kids. I'll need to recover, and you have that home inspection the day after."

"I'm sure mom can watch them," he said from our bedroom.

"I know but I don't want to keep asking her. She's not in the best of health."

"It'll be okay. Everything will work out."

"That's easy for you to say. You always to get to rest after you have surgery. I don't." I wiped Autumn's face and the two older boys charged into our bedroom to pounce on their sleepy Daddy. D.J. trailed behind them.

"Oh, hi boys." He grunted. "You could but you choose not to," he said to me.

"Really? Who is supposed to care for the kids?"

"I'll take care of them."

"No you won't. You aren't here most of the time."

"Daddy, when are you getting up?" The boys asked, interrupting our heated discussion.

"Soon...look, Lisa, I'm working. It's not like I'm at the bar or running around with friends all the time."

"I know but I just wish I could rest after I have surgeries. Sometimes I believe I'd still have to get up and work even on my deathbed!" I cried. I picked up Autumn and my thoughts turned to God, the only one who always listened and understood.

Lord, I'm trusting You to send me some friends I can have for company and for help when I need it. I know I have to be there for them too. I'm tired of doing things alone.

I underwent the surgery to repair my golf ball size hernia. To my amazement, I rested and recovered without a fight. An answer to prayer, Kathy watched the kids. I felt good except my abdomen swelled out to point of me having to wear maternity pants again and looking four months pregnant!

But I recovered just in time to care for sick kids. Their ailments passed quickly and our lives began to resemble a more normal craziness instead of a crazy, craziness for a short while.

A very short while. Our washer quit working when the transmission, seal, and belt broke. To fix the machine was not worth the cost so a family friend offered us an old washer for free. Before we received the washer, though, I still had to haul heavy baskets of clothes to the laundromat, and in doing so, I irritated my hernia repair site. To complicate matters, a wheel on the van needed repairs, the computer developed a glitch, and the toilet flooded from two cars put in by D.J. Thanks Little Man.

Once again I questioned if God wanted us to be happy and sell the house. Did He want *me* to be happy? My needs were not being met and my attitude showed it.

"Danny! Can't you get up with D.J. and Autumn in the morning once and while? I'm up with them every night while you sleep all night. I'm exhausted. I have strep throat because my body couldn't fight off the infection. I NEED SLEEP!"

Danny had been dozing off in our bed. I washed the dishes after having already finished the laundry and feeding the kids their breakfast. They were watching cartoons and playing in the living room.

"I don't hear them. Wake me up and I'll get them."

"Yeah, right. You just don't want to get up. You don't care." A few tears rolled down my cheeks.

All I want to do is get some good solid sleep. Maybe I could lose some weight and my blood pressure would go down. Maybe I wouldn't get sick.

My bad attitude prevailed into Mother's Day weekend when Danny was called in for SED, or State of Emergency Duty. My hopes of relaxing were dashed away with that one phone call. Danny repeated his belief that he shouldn't have to pamper me.

I cannot wait for him to leave for his two weeks of training!

"Oh no." I smacked my forehead. I was complaining again, exactly what I didn't want to do. "Lord, I'm angry. What I really need is for You to change me. Give me a good attitude toward my life and toward the people in it."

"Guess what Mom?" Hunter and Colt asked as they threw open the kitchen door. Danny had taken them to McDonald's and walked in behind them, shutting the door. I sat on the couch feeding Autumn her bottle while D.J. slept.

"I have no idea. Did you get a cool toy in your Happy Meal?" I said, teasing them.

"No. Daddy saved a woman from choking!"

"He did? What happened? Is the lady okay?"

"She's fine," Danny added. "I did the Heimlich Maneuver on her. She spit that fry right out. She thanked me."

"I'm impressed. Daddy is a hero isn't he?" I asked the boys.

"Yay! Daddy is a hero!" They sang and danced.

I looked at Danny. I didn't really want him to leave for two weeks. I couldn't wait for him to come home. During his time away, the kids and I enjoyed our days visiting family and playing at the park. Hunter and Colt played T-Ball. We had a pleasant time.

Upon Danny's return, I fully embraced him. My love for him had changed. God had transformed my heart. Another military wife from church invited me to join her Bible Study. The group consisted of six ladies, and we had been reading the book, A Wife After God's Own Heart by Elizabeth George. I learned that I needed to appreciate and support Danny more. If I could set aside my own desires from time to time, maybe Danny would be more receptive to me when I needed help.

Even so, Danny could only do so much. He was one person. Not only did I attend the Bible Study, I touched base with childhood friends, former coworkers, and some members of our extended family through Facebook. I had finally figured out how to use the site. Their "presence" in my life helped me not to feel totally alone. We reminisced about our past and updated each other on our present lives.

The first news I shared with them regarded my kidney stone drama. I had one on my right side. The doctor scheduled a lithotripsy procedure for October 4th, but I canceled it.

"My right side is hurting," I informed Danny that last Sunday morning in September. I sat on the edge of the bed and massaged my back on the right side. Danny looked at me from his side of the bed where he still lay, not too concerned.

"It's probably your kidney stone moving," he said.

"I hope it doesn't move too much. I will be glad to get this over with. I hate having kidney stones. I always get them after having the kids. The doctor agreed with me that the pregnancies likely caused the formation of the stones…oh man, this really hurts. It's getting worse."

No matter how I lay, stood, or sat, I felt pain. Nothing relieved it. It intensified throughout the morning. I reached a point where I couldn't handle the discomfort anymore and begged Danny to drive me to ER. I squeezed my right the side the entire time. The pressure eased some of my misery.

At the hospital, I experienced a sudden urge to use the restroom while waiting to see the doctor. Afterwards, I felt one hundred percent better. However, the ER physician administered an X-ray and CT Scan. No stone to be found.

"I don't see anything. But looking at the information from your doctor you definitely had one. Are you sure you didn't pass it?"

"You know, I used the restroom earlier. I did see a tiny rock in the toilet. Was that my stone?" I asked, raising my eyebrows. "I thought it was just in there from something else. Sorry about that."

"It probably was," he answered, sounding somewhat aggravated.

When a person says that passing a stone is worse than labor, she is right! I had the impression I could not pass mine on my own, thus the surgery. My doctor never told me I could pass it. After administering the X-ray and a CT Scan, which both showed no stone, the ER staff frowned at me when I realized I had passed the stone in the toilet there.

That explains why I felt one hundred percent better after I went to the bathroom! And that tiny "rock" in the toilet was my stone!

I apologized to the nurses but I did not intentionally create more work for nothing. What could I do but thank God.

No surgery meant no risk of high blood pressure again. I had just been taken off my blood pressure medicine prescribed to me short term. My new birth control had caused it to elevate dangerously high, or so my OB/GYN suspected. I quit taking it and lost weight again. My blood pressure returned to normal, and I wanted it to stay that way. My goals were to stay completely healthy and give myself permission to take breaks.

Earlier in the year, before connecting with old relations on Facebook and joining the Bible Study, I struggled with mood swings that even Paxil could not straighten out. Danny accused me of being crazy. In a way, he was right. Thoughts of suicide entered my mind. I talked to my doctor, who confirmed I had Postpartum Depression. To combat the illness, I took melatonin and carved out breaks for myself. Danny stayed with the kids more often.

"I'm taking two vacation days so I can help you at home. I'm sorry I haven't been here. You know I love you right?" he asked me, holding my face in his hands.

"Yes, I know. I love you to." I kissed him.

"Dear Father,

Thank You for delivering me from my health problems this year! My blood pressure is normal, my weight is better, my mood is better, and I'm free of kidney stones. You changed my attitude. I received the help I needed, not in the way I expected but nonetheless, I am making friends. I'm reaching out to others instead of waiting for You to bring them to me. I have to be a friend to have friends. Forgive me for placing all the pressure on Danny to meet my needs and on You to create all the connections. I am not alone. You are always with me. You keep Your promises even when others don't keep their word. May I forgive them just as You have forgiven me. In Jesus' name. Amen."

CHAPTER TWENTY-TWO

REJOICING AND MOURNING

"Rejoice with those who rejoice; mourn with those who mourn." Romans 12:15

"Happy Birthday Danny!" The family shouted. We had gathered at our favorite pizza place to celebrate Danny's special day. He turned the BIG 4-0! A chocolate cake, made with black lettering and icing, commemorated this momentous milestone.

"So how does it feel to reach the top of the hill?" Some of us joked.

"It doesn't bother me," Danny answered nonchalantly. He concerned himself more with spending time with family and this provided him a reason to do so.

"Remember that time when you got knocked into the hog manure pile at Aunt Blanche's?" Mike asked.

"Oh my gosh! You were covered in that stuff!" John added. The table erupted into laughter. Ah yes, visiting memory lane. Good times.

We had another chance to visit memory lane when my parents celebrated their 40th wedding anniversary June 27th. Danny and I held the party at our house. Danny grilled steak while I boiled some corn on the cob and warmed beans on the stove. I took some pictures, too. One of my favorite pictures is of my dad and mom sitting on the couch with their cake between them. I rejoiced with my parents for lasting four decades into their marriage. Not everyone has the opportunity to witness such an occasion. I hope Danny and I last that long.

Summer quickly turned into fall. Danny and I visited our families for Halloween. On the way, we drove by the place where my parents used to live and where I grew up, only to see a pile of rubble where the house once stood. "They tore down the house! I knew they would at some point since it was so run down, but I didn't think it'd be now," I said, my voice cracking.

"Mom and Dad, did you see the old house torn down?" I said, walking into their apartment. My dad sat in his usual place, the recliner.

"Yeah, we saw it the other day," My mom answered, standing in front of the hallway.

"What do you think about it? I wasn't expecting to see that. I knew they would tear it down eventually but still." I continued walking into the living with the kids next to me.

"Well, we are a little sad but it was an old house. These things happen."

"I know. It's going to seem weird driving by there and only seeing an empty lot. I'm so used to the house being there." No sense in crying over spilt milk though. I switched gears.

"Anyway, what do you think of the kids?"

"They look pretty snazzy," My dad said, smiling. "So who are you all supposed to be?"

"I'm a ninja!" Hunter said proudly.

"I'm Spider-Man!" Colt said with as much pride.

"D.J. is Thomas the Tank Engine and Autumn is Minnie Mouse." I told their Grandpa Kraft. The little Trick-or-Treaters strutted around in their fancy attire, and then followed Grandma Kraft down the hall and into the kitchen for their treats. I stayed in the living room with Dad. I sat on the floor in front of him.

"Speaking of houses, Danny and I have exciting news about a house."

"Oh yeah?"

"We put a contract on a house through a short sale about a week ago. It has three bedrooms upstairs with two more downstairs in the basement. The basement isn't totally finished, but there's a place for a bathroom. The deck is really nice and is attached to a sunroom. There's seven acres of land with it and a shop that we might purchase later. It's on property next to us that is owned by the same family. We do have neighbors, but they aren't real close. We can see them from down the road. That's what we like. The only bad thing is the house is in short sale and we have to wait for it to be approved. It should, though since we gave the highest bid of anyone at the auction."

"That's great, Lisa. I'm happy for you. You don't mind me asking, where is it?"

"It's not too far from where we are now but a little closer for Danny to drive to work. It's in Danville.

"Gotcha."

Normally I didn't have the chance to just chat with my dad because I had to chase the kids while he was relatively immobile in his chair. He no longer walked unless necessary. He suffered a stroke in 1996, which left him partially paralyzed on his left side. I treasured that time with him.

Ten days later, Danny prepared for the opening day of deer rifle season. I called him just to check in with him.

"So, you are going out in the morning right?" I asked Danny, who was finishing up a home inspection nearby.

"Yep. I'm going to buy some snacks and Gatorade, and then I will be home."

"Okay. Could you also pick up a gallon of milk and a bag of tortilla chips?"

"Will do."

"Thanks, and I need to get off of here. Alan and Paul have called me twice already. It's probably my dad."

"I love you."

"I love you too."

When I hung up the phone with Danny that afternoon, I did not panic even though Paul and Alan had both called me twice. I figured the calls related to my dad, who was possibly going to the hospital with an illness of some sort. It had happened before.

"Lisa! This is Paul. I think Dad is dead. He's not breathing. I've done CPR on him and he won't respond. Please call me!" Paul begged me in his voice message.

I listened to his words again, not believing what I heard.

"Oh no! Not my dad! Not now! Please not my dad!" I lay my head on the kitchen counter and wept uncontrollably.

When I could, I called Danny back and asked him to come home as soon as possible. He promised he would be home in a few minutes. "Sorry about your dad," he said.

Shortly after talking with Danny, he pulled into the driveway. I didn't rush out the door. Although Alan had told me Dad had a faint pulse on the way to the hospital, I already knew he was gone. Mom had called 911 when Paul couldn't help him. The paramedics tried to resuscitate him for almost an hour and they couldn't bring him back. Considering the circumstances, they suspected he died of a massive heart attack. He had suffered a minor one in 2002, which put him at a higher risk for another one. Also, the manner in which he died pointed to a massive heart attack. He had been shuffling out of the bathroom, after having just returned from Wal-Mart with Paul and my mom, when he suddenly slumped down in his chair, unresponsive.

I didn't get to say goodbye. As I studied his lifeless body on the gurney at the ER, I fought back the tears. I wanted to be strong for the others, but I missed him already. No more seeing him in his chair, or talking to him, or celebrating special moments with him. At the same time, I rejoiced in the fact that he was no longer suffering or in pain. I envisioned him running around, laughing, and smiling in heaven. I knew he was there with Preacher.

In the days to follow, I coped with my grief by looking at photos of him, writing him letters, and visiting his favorite spot at the Cuivre River's State Park's ever popular lake, Lake Lincoln. I remember sitting on one of the picnic tables, staring at the water. Nobody could see me weeping with my sunglasses on.

I wrote him a letter two days after his death on November 12, 2011:

The top reads "Raymond Herbert Kraft, September 8, 1935-November 10, 2011, 1:30pm, 76 years."

Dear Dad,

I'm writing you-something I should've done before now. I know I didn't talk to you a lot. I wanted to but didn't know what to say. I hope you knew I loved you and still do. I'm happy

187

you are at peace now. No more suffering, loneliness, or pain. You are happy, free, and healthy. You are with the Lord! That is where you were meant to be. And I will be there with you someday! But for now, I have my own family to be here for and my purpose has not been totally found. Whatever life brings me, I will do it to make you proud! I know you were proud of me already. I was so blessed to have you for almost 36 years. (That's a long time! I got to know my dad and he was in my life for a long time. Thank You Lord!)

I was proud of you too. I want to thank you for raising me to be a good person, and we didn't always agree, but that's normal. What I remember most is how hard you worked and sacrificed to give me the best. You took Paul, Alan, and me to the state park, the lock and dam, and most importantly to church. You used to play games with me, you called me Pocahontas and Tooter. You let me be a bull, running and jumping into your lap! Funny!

Many good memories. I'm glad you got to see the grandkids and see me get married. You got to celebrate 40 years of marriage with mom.

So thankful for that. I wish you could have been here for one more Christmas, but you will be in our hearts. There's a part of you in us, and we will <u>always</u> remember you. I will make sure the grandkids know about you. I know you loved them, and if they were older, they would have remembered you. That's okay. I have pictures and memories to share.

I will sure miss you. I really will. But this is only a temporary separation. I will see you later in heaven. Have fun up there! I know you are. I know they accepted you with open arms. You're with your forever family now. You finally made it to your eternal home. Praise God!

I will go. Love you.

Your little girl,
Lisa

I purchased a small container to use as a memory box. Danny gave me space to grieve that first week. I wanted to be alone, but I also wanted his comfort at least some of the time. Mostly, I just needed to know he was there for me. Later, he apologized for being distant. I give him credit for sacrificing his hunting trip on opening day of deer season, though. He stayed home with the kids so I could help my family plan the funeral.

To my disappointment, there was not enough life insurance money for an open casket, and we had to settle on cremation with a memorial service. About fifty of our friends and old acquaintances attended the memorial, which was simple but nice.

With the prayers and support of church family and friends, I survived those first few weeks of mourning my dad. I kept thinking about all the things he would never see. He would not see Autumn's first birthday, our new house, or my new, much shorter haircut. However, I was blessed to have him as long as I did.

We still celebrated Thanksgiving and Christmas with extended family as we did every year. I bought my mom an ornament for her tree that could hold a picture of her beloved husband. We enjoyed being together but the room felt empty without Dad.

I knew life had to go on, but I struggled to find joy again. I had to stop myself from crying at the dentist's office when he fixed my new bridge that December. Should I have canceled the appointment? No, because my dad had wanted me to be happy and take care of myself. He would want me to live my life. A new year was fast approaching and I was ready. I wanted to focus on living in freedom for 2012. God had more in store for me, waiting to be seen.

"Dear Father,

Thank You for Danny's birthday, my parents' anniversary party, and most importantly, my dad's life. I miss him tremendously! Forgive me for not talking to him more. I'm sure he knew I loved him either way. He understood my crazy, busy life with four kids. Help me treasure time with my family and to live in such a way that makes Dad proud.

I don't want to live the life he had. Seeing him suffer from a stroke and two heart attacks reminds me I need to relax more. I'm better, but I still have moments of anger and anxiety. I don't want to be so high strung. I need Your help. In Jesus' name. Amen."

CHAPTER TWENTY-THREE

A NEW HOME

"Now to him who is able to do immeasurably more than all we ask or imagine, according to his power that is at work within us..." Ephesians 3:20

"Enlarge the place of your tent, stretch your tent curtains wide, do not hold back; lengthen your cords, strengthen your stakes. For you will spread out to the right and to the left; your descendants will dispossess nations and settle in their desolate cities." Isaiah 54:2-3

"Whew! It sure is hot today." I wiped the sweat off my forehead. Stacks of boxes were piled up by the door.

"Put that box over there," I heard Alan from inside the moving truck instruct one of Danny's friends.

"Lisa, what do you want me to do with this?" Paul asked holding out an old mop.

"Uh, throw it away. I don't need it." Moving day! A chance to start fresh! Throw out the old and keep the new. I couldn't believe this day had finally come.

Danny and I wondered if God was ever going to provide a bigger house for us, especially after the contract on the second house fell through. The seller's bank kept us in suspense for what seemed like years but in reality was four months. We received the devastating news toward the end of February.

"Fine! We will live in this little, cramped house forever! You don't care! Forget looking for houses anymore. What's the point?" I angrily told God.

God spoke to me in that still, small voice to say we needed to look further out, or in other words, closer to Danny's job. Two weeks later, while in the midst of finding a load for Alan, I squeezed in a few moments of house hunting. I suddenly spotted it. THE house.

"Four bedrooms, three bathrooms, two fireplaces, a finished basement, and almost four acres of land AND close to Danny's job, too. Perfect!"

I was excited while also cautiously optimistic. I had also discovered a couple of other houses as potential homes for us so Danny and I planned a day to look at all of them. Would one of them be the right house?

We loaded up the four kids and stopped at Hermann to taste delicious varieties of sausages at the Wurstfest. Then we visited the three houses. I liked certain aspects of each home, but the brick one stood out. It was perfect for us. The seller, who was a dear lady in her sixties, agreed to a price we could afford and "voila", the house was ours!

Danny and I signed the contract at the end of March and both parties agreed to wait until after school finished before closing on the deal. This arrangement worked out well for us because we had time to pack and sell our old home. Danny rented a storage unit close to the new one so we could pack a little at a time. By clearing our old home of clutter, we could present a better package, as one might say to interested buyers.

Our real estate agent brought a young couple by to see our house, and they wanted it. We disputed the selling price but finally settled on a number. Danny and I were a bit disappointed because we would have to pay about $200-$400 to get out from under it, but we sold our propane to offset the costs. Our old house was sold and we had only one house payment! The details fell into place. God had come through for us more than we imagined.

My family was happy for us. They did not want us to move further away, but we assured them we would visit. Danny's family, on the other hand, expressed their concerns. I did feel bad leaving Kathy with her recent cancer diagnosis. However, the other family members had to understand our reasons.

Before we actually moved that summer, we had so much to finish, including minor repairs and family celebrations. Autumn, Hunter, and D.J. celebrated their birthdays one last time at the old house. Autumn had her first birthday there. Most of our family came to watch the baby girl open her presents, which included dolls, clothes, and books. Her bear cake was made by the local bakery. She dug into the sweet, tasty treat without hesitation.

Hunter's 8th birthday did not involve extended family as did Autumn's, but we let him invite a friend to go bowling with us. Hunter received the gifts he asked for, and I created a snake cake, decorated with green icing and two toy snakes.

D.J.'s 3rd birthday was packed full of activities being that it was close to Easter. Extended family came to celebrate the Little Man and the resurrection of our Savior. The sun shone warmly on us as the kids rode bikes, played basketball and golf, hunted eggs, talked to each other, and swung on the swing set. D.J. played with his new toys and ate his yummy Chuggington cake baked by yours truly. We extended the celebration to another day where he could enjoy a day at the Museum of Transportation. What better place to take a train-loving three year old?

We celebrated Colt's baptism as well. When he was submerged in the baptismal water, his top half dunked under the water and his feet popped up above it! I couldn't help but laugh. It was pure joy, seeing him publicly confess his faith, the same as his big brother.

For Mother's Day, Danny and I treated our moms to lunch out at the Olive Garden. My mom had never been to the Italian restaurant. Both moms appreciated the gift and the time they had with us. We knew our visits would be limited after the move.

Packing all of our items proved to be challenging for me when Danny had to be gone at the end of May for two weeks and at the beginning of June for two more weeks to complete some training.

"Lord, help me keep up with all the activities going on and help me get the packing done." I had prayed during this extra busy time.

Hunter and Colt had T-Ball games and summer school. Their Scout pack had their Blue and Gold Banquet and Pinewood Derby. Both boys received numerous badges and awards. Hunter still played the fiddle.

D.J. qualified for language therapy and started attending his special preschool. I hoped this would be the key to open his voice.

Doctor and dentist appointments had to be scheduled and attended before the move too.

I even squeezed in an appointment with a friend of mine who cut my hair into layers and showed me another way to apply my makeup. I figured, "What better time for getting a fresh look than with this new chapter in my life?"

Besides having God by my side, what helped me endure upcoming big change was not having to search for truck loads. Alan had closed down his business. He lost too much money. With that income loss, I appreciated the flood of home inspections Danny had to do. Of course this meant we barely had time for each other, but we made time, especially for special occasions like Valentine's Day and his birthday.

While happy for the prospect of a new life, the stress of it was overwhelming. My patience was reduced to almost non-existence. It wasn't a surprise that I overreacted when one of the scout leaders harped on my boys' failures, while bragging about her son's accomplishments at the Cub Scout day camp. I glared at her.

Excuse me! We don't have time to fish and swim like you! You don't know what it's like to be a military family where one parent is gone all the time.

I talked to the Cub Master and posted my thoughts on Facebook, intentionally where this "Parent of the Year" could read it. Predictably, she confronted me about it. We both apologized and made amends. She didn't intend to make me feel bad and her days had been stressful too.

What I learned is that I could not focus on myself all the time. I had to consider other's struggles and forgive them for messing up. Bitterness and anger causes relationship problems, not just for acquaintances, but friends and family too.

That day that I had snapped back over the silly comments had been preceded by a scary and yet-more-stress inducing event. Just two weeks prior to that incident, I had hit a deer with the van. Less than five miles from the house on the way to Hunter's fiddle lesson, BAM! Two deer were there right over the top of the hill. I could either hit them or drive off the road into the ditch. On impact, I had been traveling at about 55mph and the hood flew up where I couldn't even see the road! It fell back down as I came to a stop.

I shook from fright, and feared the kids' reactions. They laughed, believe it or not. They aren't scared of much it seems.

I pulled myself together enough to slowly turn the van around and limp it back home. We never drove it again. The insurance totaled it. We used the business van after that incident, and we purchased a 1991 Dodge Dynasty with the insurance money.

My life seemed to be falling apart the closer the time for the move came. I told myself in my journal that,

> *"I really need to get in my 'happy place'. With so much to do it's easy to get stressed out and over react. I want to be happy and calm even during chaos. I don't want to be complaining and getting upset over everything. I've asked God to help me. It's all I can do. I'm just glad we are almost thru our 'big change'. One more month. June is going to be interesting..."*

I prayed for the move to our new home, hoping it would bring positive changes. Our family had to find new doctors, the boys had to navigate their way around new schools, and we had to familiarize ourselves with a new area. We were ready for the change, though. We had already found a church. The pastor had been the children's church pastor at our other church. Since we knew him, we felt the transition would be fairly easy for the whole family.

As for me, I wanted to find some good friends and possibly a Christian couple to be godparents for the kids. I wanted a couple who were attending church regularly and who could be good role models to the kids in all areas, especially being responsible with money and resources. The couple needed to have a true concern for our kids and want to be with them.

So there I was on moving day, June 23^{rd,} full of anticipation. Our new babysitter kept D.J. and Autumn busy and out of the way, while Alan, Paul, and some of Danny's coworkers successfully packed and transported our items. Alan ensured a smooth move for us since he had previously worked for a moving company. The day was exhausting but exciting. I spent the next two weeks unpacking, unpacking, and unpacking! I lost about five pounds in the process.

The kids explored our new home and adjusted to their new surroundings with ease. We maintained our normal routine. D.J. had no problem running through the house butt-naked after baths as he always had. Autumn carried around her Mr. Bear and drank from her bottle. Hunter and Colt watched television and played outside in the big back yard. At night, I still read to all the kids. I always made sure I connected with them, if not fully during the day, at least at night before they went to bed. They would gather around me and listen to the stories, then off to dreamland.

Before the move, Tina, who I mentioned before, took pictures of the kids (her future godchildren) at the old house for memory's sake. Danny and I took pictures of all of us on the day we closed on it. I admit I missed the house with all its memories. At the same time, however, we needed to make new memories at our new house.

We watched fireworks on the riverfront for Independence Day and celebrated Colt's 7th birthday. For the Birthday Boy's special day, we visited the nature center. All the kids admired the live animals, and Hunter fulfilled his dream of holding a live snake. His face beamed. In addition, we ate at two restaurants and Danny barbecued. How nice to have some fun after all the hard work.

We had settled into our new lives, and I could not have been more content.

"Dear Father,

Thank You for our new home. I love it. It's just what I wanted. The kids like it with the big yard and the extra space inside. It's the perfect size. Forgive me for accusing You of not caring or wanting to answer our need. I'm sorry for letting stress rule my actions. You knew what You were doing all along, even as far back as seven years ago when I first prayed for a new home. Thank You that everything fell into place. Thank You for all the help with the move, which made for a smooth transition too. We have nice neighbors, great schools and wonderful new doctors. Thank You! Please show us what our new roles are in our new place. In Jesus' name. Amen."

CHAPTER TWENTY-FOUR

NEW PEOPLE, NEW HOPE

"As iron sharpens iron, so one man sharpens another."
Proverbs 27:17

"A new command I give you: Love one another. As
I have loved you, so you must love one another."
John 13:34

There sure are a lot of weeds. Will I ever get done? My hands and back are killing me! If only I didn't have to do this or there was an easier way. Of course I pick the hottest part of the day. I'll be so glad to get this done and settle in.

I bent over tugging the overgrown weeds behind the house. Some of them reached up to my shoulders. My clothes were drenched in sweat, a lovely sight I'm sure.

"Hello?" A lady's voice called.

I looked up to see my new neighbors. The lady was holding a plate of cookies and a bottle of wine. Next to her stood her husband and two kids, a boy and a girl.

"Oh hi. Sorry I'm such a mess. I'm trying to clean up these weeds."

"That's okay. We understand. I'm Jenny and this is Cory, Audrey, and Jesse. We wanted to give you a little welcome gift. The kids couldn't wait to meet you!" Jenny laughed.

"It's nice to meet you. The kids are inside. Their names are Hunter, Colt, D.J, and Autumn. I'm Lisa and my husband is Danny. Thank you for the gift. I'll take this inside and tell the kids you are out here. They are excited to meet you too."

The kids played with Jesse outside, who happened to be four days younger than Colt. Jenny and I talked about our families and interesting facts about the area as we watched them. Cory and Audrey had gone back home with chores to do. Audrey was twelve and almost ready to babysit. She had recently completed a babysitting course. (Yes! A babysitter who is CPR trained.) Jenny told me the elementary school assigned to our kids was one of the best in the district. The more Jenny and I talked, the more I realized God had answered our prayers in every way possible. He exceeded my expectations.

With new neighbors and other new people, my hope soared to the clouds. I began to see new possibilities and new adventures to enhance our lives. I wanted to be a blessing to these people too.

Summer passed quickly. On the first day of school, I wondered all day about the boys. Did they like their new schools? Were they making friends? Were their teachers nice? Would they have a good first day? If their first day didn't go well, how would that impact the rest of the year?

At the time the busses were due to arrive, I waited anxiously, wanting to hear the news. D.J. came home first. He went only half days. The big smile on his face said it all. He couldn't tell me about his day, but his teacher wrote a note saying, "D.J. did great!" Then Hunter and Colt's bus came later in the afternoon.

"So? How was your day?" I asked as soon as they stepped off the bus.

"We love it!" The both said at the same time. They jabbered about how they loved their teachers and their classes. They met new friends.

"I'm happy for you. Are you glad we moved?"

"Uh...yeah!" Hunter replied.

"Do you want to go back to your old school?" I joked.

"No way! We like it here and we want to stay."

"Good, because we aren't going anywhere for a while," I reassured them.

No more worries about the boys liking school.

Another fear disappeared when D.J. began talking. His special education teacher and therapist found ways to unlock his voice. However, with his newfound voice arose other concerns. His intelligibility, or how well other people understood him, appeared to be significantly delayed.

"Lisa, the reason I want to re-evaluate D.J. is I think he might have apraxia," the therapist said at the re-evaluation meeting.

Apraxia? No way!

This newly discovered speech and motor planning disorder causes misfires in the brain, which control muscle movement. Even muscles in the mouth are affected. Children display various symptoms that include groping of the mouth, fine motor delays, and the loss of acquired skills. I had just learned about the disorder from researching speech delays for a writing assignment and now my son may have it?

"What does this mean?" I asked, shocked and confused. "I thought he simply had a speech delay."

"All it means it that he will require a different approach to learning his speech sounds."

"Will he be able to talk normal and function in a regular classroom when he goes to kindergarten?"

"Most likely. He's only three and a half. He has nearly two years in the program here to make progress. I've seen kids do very well. Every kid is different, depending on the severity and the willingness to learn. Cooperation is a key factor here. After working with D.J., I don't see that being a problem. He should do fine."

"I'm sure you're right. I'm just surprised. Please do what you have to do. I want what is best for D.J."

As suspected, the results of the evaluation indicated D.J. had apraxia-like symptoms. With a clearer picture as to what was wrong with my little boy, he could finally get the help he needed. Over the course of the school year, with his speech/language therapy and occupational therapy, he talked in complete sentences that could be understood by others, and he learned to cut with scissors, draw, and use the toilet on occasion.

With his newfound voice, he came out with some cute (and inventive) phrases. Here are some of my favorites:

"Cookie" for Coltie.

"When you get bigga, I get bigga bigga, and that's the bigga bigga truth!"

"Lickalicious" to describe yummy food.

"Baby Bye...Baby Autumn! You're so cute and helpful."

Autumn disliked the last one. She'd cry and yell at her big brother, "I'm not a baby!" She was right. She was using the toilet at home and saying a few words too. I had been worried she'd have apraxia but then eventually she vocalized her wants, and at an earlier age than D.J.

Now what if we hadn't moved here? Did the other therapist know about apraxia? Would D.J. have received the correct diagnosis and the right therapy? How grateful I am that his current therapist knew about the speech disorder. Coincidence? I don't think so. I finally have validation for why D.J. didn't talk. No one can accuse me of not working with him, making me feel like a bad mom. No more hearing

people suggest he has autism or that he is a "late talker."
Praise you Lord!

My encounters with neighbors, teachers, and therapists gave me new hope. They offered a fresh perspective on my life. The care and love shown by them encouraged me to step out of my comfort zone more. I wanted to be a loving neighbor and become a better person because of them.

"Dear Father,

I am speechless! (Funny how I would say that when D.J. spent his first three and a half years unable to verbalize his wants.) How is it that this move was the answer to several prayers? You really do know what I need. My hope is renewed. Sorry for being impatient and for worrying. I'm still working on trusting You. I ask that You help me change and that these new people can help me get there. I want to be a loving neighbor and friend. I want You to continue showing me new ideas and my new purpose here. In Jesus' name. Amen."

CHAPTER TWENTY-FIVE

A NEW MINDSET

"Therefore, I urge you, brothers, in view of God's mercy, to offer your bodies as living sacrifices, holy and pleasing to God—this is your spiritual act of worship. Do not conform any longer to the pattern of this world, but be transformed by the renewing of your mind. Then you will be able to test and approve what God's will is— his good, pleasing and perfect will." Romans 12:1-2

"Therefore, if anyone is in Christ, he is a new creation: the old has gone, the new has come!" 2 Corinthians 5:17

"Hi. How are you?" I greeted the other church members with hugs and smiles. I placed my Bible and notebook on a chair in front of the small, but cozy sanctuary. Then I walked around talking with everyone there. I loved my church family. They had become an important asset in changing my mindset. I wanted to think more like Christ and needed the right teaching for me to accomplish that.

Our leader, Pastor Larry, boldly taught us the truth and encouraged us to grow. He always said, "Pray using Scripture. Speak His Word." I did not merely show up to service anymore. With a much smaller congregation, I accepted my part as the Body of Christ in a way I had not done before.

Pastor Larry led us to pray for each other and read the Bible every day. His guidance motivated me to face my weaknesses head on, even my emotional weaknesses. It was time to wean off my Paxil. The antidepressant was never meant to be taken long term, and certainly not for ten years, as in my case.

The first visit to my new family doctor involved the discussion to do just that, yet still be freed from the chains of anxiety and anger. He said, "Medication is one-third of the solution. It only treats the symptoms, not the cause. You need to see a therapist. Therapy is two-thirds of the solution. Here's the name of a good one here in town, but of course you can use whoever you want."

A therapist? I don't want to see a therapist! I'm a Christian. I shouldn't need one. Shouldn't my faith be strong enough to defeat this giant? People will think I'm crazy. Danny was right. I AM crazy!

Reluctantly I called the office to set up an appointment with the "crazy person" doctor. I didn't know what to expect. Would I be lying on a couch pouring out my problems while he sat in his chair taking notes? Would he ask me about my childhood? Would I be sobbing while he comforted me? Or even worse, would he say I was crazy?

While he did sit in a chair, I wasn't lying on a couch. I sat in a chair across from him and he let me say whatever was on my mind.

"I'm upset with my family because they don't seem to care about seeing us. Whenever we go to visit my mom, no one else stops by to see us. Then there's my son, Hunter. He aggressively attacks his brother Colt, and he throws tantrums when the situation at hand does not go the way he hopes. He throws his toys, rips the sheets off his bed, and tears up his books. I haven't handled stress the best way at times, and I wonder if he picked up those strong reactions from me. I want to handle stress better, and I want to get weaned off my Paxil."

"So how long have you been taking Paxil?"

"Ten years...I know that is a long time. None of my other doctors ever suggested I see someone like you. My husband, Danny, has told me I'm crazy and I need to see a psychiatrist. I guess he was right," I admitted.

"Well, you aren't crazy. You just need some help. Let me help guide you. First, don't worry about those people who don't want to see you. Focus on seeing your mom. For Hunter, develop a behavior plan. Discuss consequences for his choices. Make sure you aren't reinforcing negative behavior. Don't ignore it. But don't give it unnecessary attention...Do you think he wants attention?"

"Quite possibly. He's always sought out more attention than the other kids and has acted out more when he's not receiving it, but I can't just ignore everyone else so he can get all my time."

"I understand that. See what you can do. Ask him to help you with chores. He'll feel important."

"Okay. I'll try it."

"That's good. I'd like to see you in a couple of weeks."

"Sure."

Over the next six months, I poured out my frustrations with the therapist. He listened to me vent and offered suggestions on how to cope or respond.

As I reflected on those sessions and on Hunter's behavior, I examined my own actions. Could it have been in how I treated him that caused him to misbehave? Had I shown genuine care and love to him? I had to answer no. In all honesty, Hunter still annoyed me. Even though I didn't say my thoughts out loud, Hunter had sensed it. I vowed from then on to love Hunter and to view him as the terrific kid everyone else recognized.

"Hunter, I'm sorry if I haven't loved you as you deserve. I don't know why I haven't treated you better. You really are a great kid. Forgive me?" I handed Hunter a cup to rinse off.

"Maybe." He grinned at me and held out his hand for another cup to rinse.

"Are we good?"

"Maybe."

Hunter's behavior gradually improved. Whenever he felt the urge to lash out at Colt or break something, he came to

Danny or me. We discussed the issue and resolved it with the best solution possible. Danny told Hunter he was not allowed to act aggressively in our home anymore. We expected him to control his emotions and his behaviors.

God had also prompted me to apologize to other people I had hurt with my words. I wrote my sister-in-law a letter about a misunderstanding we'd had, and I sent messages to Facebook friends. Regardless of what people did or didn't do, I needed to speak only words that were useful for God's kingdom. Once I repented of my wrongdoings, a sense of freedom came over me. A heavy burden had been lifted off my shoulders. I could be a true friend.

With these new people in my life, I realized I had to be ready for friendship. Before the move, I wasn't in the right place. I had to be willing to fully give of myself. "To have friends one must be a friend" is true. I had to let go of situations I had no control over. I had to forgive my transgressors and most importantly myself. The enemy had me convinced I wasn't worth God's forgiveness. The guilt plagued me every time my past crept back into my thoughts. I had focused on my problems instead of reaching out to others, including my own family.

I couldn't believe I acted the way I did at times. Why did I allow worry and anger in? Why did I allow pride in? Why did I shut others out with my negative attitude? Why did I shut out God? He wanted to bless me and answer my prayers, but not if I didn't let Him. I had to rely on Him and His Word without trying to solve everything on my own understanding. How much easier to lay my life at his feet! How much more could I be the loving mom to my kids when I let His love rule my life?

Over the course of time, I learned to rely on Him more and handle stress better. I weaned off the Paxil. I gained confidence in myself; that is until God allowed one more test to cross my path in the area of finances. After all the provisions He had given me, I still doubted His willingness to meet my material needs. Could I move up to a new level of faith when I hit rock bottom?

"Dear Father,

Thank You for opening my eyes to the truth of Your Word. It has been there all along and I simply needed the right people to guide me in the right direction. These people encouraged me and showed me how to change my thinking. The enemy had used my thoughts to lie to me, telling me I should worry about circumstances out of my control, that I should hold onto guilt, that I am not forgiven, that I didn't deserve friends. He convinced me I had to be angry and fearful. No more! I'm a new creation. The old things are gone and the new things have come. I will cling to You. I will love others the way You have loved me, even when the love isn't deserved. Help me be more like You. In Jesus' precious name. Amen."

CHAPTER TWENTY-SIX

A NEW LEVEL OF FAITH

"Perseverance must finish its work so that you may be mature and complete, not lacking anything." James 1:4

"He will have no fear of bad news; his heart is steadfast, trusting in the Lord." Psalm 112:7

"Lord,

I am having trouble with our finances. It seems we are going in debt instead of getting out of debt. I want to get out of debt, pay off credit card, school loans, and put our house on a fifteen year loan. I also want to have money to save. I don't know what to do. You are the only one who can help me (us). Please show me what I need to do and to change. I know there's a way somewhere, somehow. Only

You know. Help me hear Your voice. Help me trust You. I'm claiming the promise of Your blessings. We have been tithing so now I'm claiming Your blessing as Malachi 3:10 says. Let the floodgates of heaven open! In Jesus' name. Amen."

I wrote this letter toward the beginning of 2013. We used the credit card to compensate for income loss. The real estate agent no longer called Danny to do home inspections.

"It'd sure be nice if you could get some home inspections again. I wonder why they quit calling," I said to Danny. I filled out checks at the kitchen table and he made coffee.

"I don't know. I'd like to get some too."

"Have you tried calling them?"

"No. I know I should."

"I would've thought with having Mondays off they would use you more."

"I know, but it is during the slow period. I'll call them soon."

"All right."

I don't know why he won't call them. Does he not care about our finances?

A few days later, Danny contacted the real estate agent. She had misunderstood him. She thought he was not doing inspections anymore, and the office staff found other inspectors to take his place. We had to cancel our business insurance. That agent charged us half of the policy value despite the fact they had been late completing the policy and it only covered a month. That hurt.

Then, as if we hadn't suffered enough financial hardship, later in the year Danny was put on furlough twice. The first time lasted only five days and he worked on orders, so we didn't lose money that time necessarily. Even though we didn't lose money with the second furlough either, his pay was delayed until the government reopened. In addition to the furloughs, Danny lost his VA benefits for three months. We depended on that money to pay our mortgage.

"Can we pay this bill late?" I begged the mortgage company, the electric company, and other creditors.

"Yes. That will not be a problem. Sorry you are having such a hard time," they replied. What a blessing to have understanding creditors.

In addition to the availability of the credit card and the sympathy of our creditors, we survived by using our income tax return money and accepting the help of others. We used our tax return to replace the broken down dishwasher, rebuild our rotting deck, put tile in the bathroom downstairs, and maintain the vehicles.

Danny's brothers hired him for side jobs, such as trimming trees and staining a deck. A few church members generously offered us groceries, clothes, free school pictures, and money to help as well. Plus through God's leading, we sold our car and some scrap. I'll never forget that night when God literally told me to, "Sell the car." I heard what sounded to me like an audible voice. Danny questioned what I heard until the car sold.

There was a flurry of home inspections scheduled right before Christmas. We may not have seen many during the year but we saw an explosion of them just in time to provide the money we needed for Danny and me to play Santa. I enjoyed watching the joy in the kids' faces as they opened their gifts. Priceless. They had been so good during the time of our financial losses. When we walked through stores looking at toys for Christmas, if Hunter, Colt, D.J., or Autumn asked for toy, even a small one, I had to say no. Yet, they did not cry or throw a fit. I told them they would get these toys eventually. Santa would not forget their patience.

Another avenue of God's provisions opened up. My writing career looked promising. I finished my writing course and received a diploma. I submitted one of my assignments to a magazine and they accepted it. My first published piece!

When I first submitted the story and the associate editor asked me to change the wording and some of the information, I almost walked away from the assignment. My pride was wounded but God prompted me to revise the article, and I completed the changes. I'm glad I listened to Him and the editor.

At the start of 2014, Danny had been assigned to attend a school with the Guard in North Dakota for one month. I was a nervous wreck those first few days! A massive winter storm had hit our state which brought snow, dangerously cold temperatures, and wind gusts up to 30-40 mph. I added wood to the fireplaces continuously for three days. The kids and I were cooped up in the house, growing more stir-crazy by the minute. My friends and family checked on us, and I called my mom every one of those days.

By the middle of that week, the weather improved and I breathed a sigh of relief. I would survive until Danny returned. I would be fine and so would our finances.

We received extra money from Danny's trip. God had told me 2014 would be a "Year of Holy Prosperity" and I claimed it. He would bless us because we had been obedient. He's my source for everything and He provides abundance to His children when they humble themselves before Him. He wanted to use Danny and me to bless others and we could only do that if we were in a position to do so.

Our finances improved because we had prayed constantly. Our family, friends and church family had earnestly prayed for us too. To be surrounded by prayer and love of others brought complete peace and comfort.

Lord, this is what it's all about. Reaching out to others and to You. I am amazed at how You carried us through this difficult time. We couldn't have done it without You or our prayer warriors. I am grateful beyond words.

Through the prayers and Scriptures we learned through the "21 Days to Your Debt Freedom" series by Gloria Copeland and Pastor George Pearsons (found at www.kcm. org), we witnessed a turnaround. God showed me a floodgate opening to indicate that financial prosperity was on the way. He wanted us to fully trust Him through our trials and we did just that. We had no other choice. Once we placed our trust Him, He could do His part.

"Dear Father,

You never cease to amaze me! You carried us through our biggest trial yet. I look back to 2013 and wonder, "How did we survive?" It was all You. You provided everything we needed when we needed it, and You showed us what to do. Other people stepped up to help us as well. We couldn't have done it without them following Your prompting. My faith has been stretched, which is good. I can honestly say that I have learned to fully rely on You for every area of my life, now that I know how. Using Scripture, or in other words, applying Your promises, is the key. Now I can focus on loving my kids instead of my problems. I don't have to panic, throw a fit, or be hateful to my loved ones when a conflict arises. I go to You first. I ask for help. Then I do what I need to do to make it happen. Please help me keep my faith in You, especially during hardship. May I never forget what I learned this past year, or during the last ten years. In Jesus' name. Amen."

CONCLUSION

NO MORE BABIES!

"And the child grew and became strong; he was filled
with wisdom, and the grace of God was on him."
Luke 2:40

"Praise the LORD. Blessed is the man who fears the
LORD, who finds great delight in his commands. His
children will be mighty in the land; the generation of
the upright will be blessed." Psalm 112:1

"**Y**ou are two handfuls," I told Hunter, holding up all
ten fingers. "What am I going to do with you now?"

"I don't know," he answered, smiling.

"I know. It means I have to love you even more!" I tried to
hug him but he squirmed away. Too big for the mushy stuff.

I loved Hunter more than the day he was born. I never
thought I would see this day. When I brought him home from

the hospital, Kathy warned me the time with him would speed by. *Yeah right!* I'd thought. But she was right.

He excelled in school, testing high enough for admittance into the gifted program. No more boredom at school. He was a smart cookie, and so talented! He and Colt received numerous awards during the character assembly at school. Colt had been dismissed from speech therapy as well.

For Cub Scouts, both boys earned several pins, belt loops and their badges at the Blue and Gold Banquet. Hunter was officially a Webelo and Colt was officially a Bear.

I gained insight into D.J.'s speech disorder when I read Speaking of Apraxia by Leslie A. Lindsay, R.N., B.SN., and when I joined two Facebook groups: CASANA, or Childhood Apraxia of Speech Association of North America, and APRAXIA KIDS-Every Child Deserves a Voice. Connecting with other parents, who had the same struggles, helped me cope with D.J.

My Little Man wore underwear during the day finally. I tried a new strategy involving the switching out of treats, frequent toilet breaks, wearing underwear at home, and cutting back on liquids. There were those occasional accidents, but I was beginning to see the light at the end of the tunnel. My days of changing diapers were coming to an end.

And guess what? Right at the beginning of 2014, I reached that light at the end of that tunnel. Autumn used the toilet everywhere we went, and the doctor had discovered

D.J. was severely constipated. For two and half months, D.J. took Miralax.

That day at the doctor's office, when D.J. saw the X-ray of his colon and heard the doctor explain his problem, he began to use the toilet for every bathroom need from then on, even before taking the stool softener.

With Hunter just turning ten that February, my decade of diapers had ended. No more babies. Even Autumn knew she was growing up. She slept in a regular bed, and she no longer drank from a bottle. Her speech and language appeared slightly delayed but she could still say, "I'm not a baby anymore!"

"Dear Father,

I never thought I'd see the day when I would stop changing diapers, yet it finally came. I can look back on the last ten years with satisfaction. I made many mistakes, but I learned and grew from them. The enemy's lies that told me I shouldn't ask for help and that I should do things on my own, no longer control my life. I let You in and the lies were pushed out. I can love my kids and be the mom I want to be. I learned to trust You, my heavenly Father, for every step of the way. My faith strengthened from all the hardships.

You were there for every diaper change, for every sickness, and for every new milestone. Just as my kids are growing up, I am growing up in Christ. I am blessed beyond measure and I am ready for whatever the next ten years bring my way. I will continue raising my children Your way. They are no longer babies, but I am ready for the next decade and beyond with them.

The teenage years are soon upon me. I'll definitely need You for that! In Jesus' name. Amen".

SCRIPTURES TO STUDY FOR BIBLE STUDIES AND PERSONAL DEVOTIONALS

≈

ANGER/TEMPER:

"For his (the LORD's) anger lasts only a moment, but his favor lasts a lifetime..." Psalm 30:5a

"A fool gives full vent to his anger, but a wise man keeps himself under control." Proverbs 29:11

"My dear brothers, take note of this: Everyone should be quick to listen, slow to speak and slow to become angry, for man's anger does not bring about the righteous life that God desires." James 1:19-20

"Do not make friends with a hot-tempered man, do not associate with one easily angered, or you may learn his ways and get yourself ensnared." Proverbs 22:24-25

"'In your anger do not sin': Do not let the sun go down while you are still angry, and do not give the devil a foothold." Ephesians 4:26-27

ANXIETY/DEPRESSION:

"An anxious heart weighs a man down, but a kind word cheers him up." Proverbs 12:25

"So do not worry, saying, 'What shall we eat?" or 'What shall we drink?' or 'What shall we wear?' For the pagans run after all these things, and your Heavenly Father knows that you need them. But seek first his kingdom and his righteousness, and all these things will be given to you as well. Therefore, do not worry about tomorrow, for tomorrow will worry about itself. Each day has enough trouble of its own." Matthew 6:31-34

"Do not be anxious about anything, but in everything, by prayer and petition, with thanksgiving, present your requests to God. And the peace of God, which transcends all understanding, will guard your hearts and your minds in Christ Jesus. Philippians 4:6-7

"Cast all your anxiety on him because he cares for you." 1 Peter 5:7

FAITH:

"Now faith is being sure of what we hope for and certain of what we do not see." Hebrews 11:1

"He replied, 'Because you have so little faith. I tell you the truth, if you have faith as small as a mustard seed, you can say to this mountain, 'Move from here to there' and it will move. Nothing will be impossible for you.'" Matthew 17:20

"Consequently, faith comes from hearing the message, and the message is heard through the word of Christ." Romans 10:17

"Be joyful in hope, patient in affliction, faithful in prayer." Romans 12:12

"The LORD will fulfill his purpose for me; your love, O LORD, endures forever-do not abandon the works of your hands." Psalm 138:8

FINANCES:

"Misfortune pursues the sinner, but prosperity is the reward of the righteous." Proverbs 13:21

"A greedy man stirs up dissension, but he who trusts in the LORD will prosper." Proverbs 28:25

"'Bring in the whole tithe into the storehouse, that there may be food in my house. Test me in this,' says the LORD Almighty, 'and see if I will throw open the floodgates of heaven and pour out so much blessing that you will not have room enough for it.'" Malachi 3:10

"Do not be like them (hypocrites), for your Father knows what you need before you ask him." Matthew 6:8

"And my God will meet all your needs according to his glorious riches in Christ Jesus." Philippians 4:19

"Give and it will be given to you. A good measure, pressed down, shaken together and running over, will be poured into your lap. For with the measure you use, it will be measured to you." Luke 6:38

GODLY RELATIONSHIPS:

"Children, obey your parents in the Lord, for this is right. 'Honor your father and mother'-which is the first commandment with a promise-'that it may go well with you and that you may enjoy long life on earth.'" Ephesians 6:1-3

"Do not be yoked together with unbelievers. For what do righteousness and wickedness have in common? Or what fellowship can light have with darkness?" 2 Corinthians 6:14

"Flee from sexual immorality. All other sins a man commits are outside his body, but he who sins sexually sins against his own body." 1 Corinthians 6:18

"And let us consider how we may spur one another on toward love and good deeds. Let us not give up meeting together, as some are in the habit of doing, but let us encourage one another-and all the more as you see the Day approaching." Hebrews 10:24-25

"A man of many companions may come to ruin, but there is a friend who sticks closer than brother." Proverbs 18:24

"He who walks with the wise grows wise, but a companion of fools suffers harm." Proverbs 13:20

GUILT:

"...let us draw near to God with a sincere heart in full assurance of faith, having our hearts sprinkled to cleanse us from a guilty conscience and having our bodies washed with pure water." Hebrews 10:22

"In him we have redemption through his blood, the forgiveness of sins, in accordance with the riches of God's grace that he lavished on us with all wisdom and understanding." Ephesians 1:7-8

"If we confess our sins, he is faithful and just and will forgive us our sins and purify us from all unrighteousness." 1 John 1:9

"Therefore, there is now no condemnation for those who are in Christ Jesus, because through Christ Jesus the law of the Spirit of life set me free from the law of sin and death." Romans 8:1-2

HEALTH/HEALING:

"Do not be wise in your own eyes; fear the LORD and shun evil. This will bring health to your body and nourishment to your bones." Proverbs 3:7-8

"But he was pierced for our transgressions, he was crushed for iniquities; the punishment that brought us peace was upon him, and by his wounds we are healed." Isaiah 53:5

"Jesus turned and saw her, 'Take heart, daughter,' he said, 'your faith has healed you.' And the woman was healed from that moment." Matthew 9:22

"Therefore confess your sins to each other and pray for each other so that you may be healed. The prayer of a righteous man is powerful and effective." James 5:16

HONESTY:

"LORD, who may dwell in your sanctuary? Who may live on your holy hill? He whose walk is blameless and who does what is righteous, who speaks the truth from his heart..." Psalm 15:1-2

"Yet a time is coming and has now come when the true worshipers will worship the Father in spirit and truth, for they are the kind of worshipers the Father seeks. God is spirit, and his worshipers must worship in spirit and in truth." John 4:23-24

"'Do not use dishonest standards when measuring length, weight or quantity. Use honest scales and honest weights, an honest ephah and an honest hin." Leviticus 19:35-36

"You shall not give false testimony against your neighbor." Exodus 20:16

"The law of the LORD is perfect, reviving the soul. The statutes of the LORD are trustworthy, making wise the simple." Psalm 19:7

HOPE/ENCOURAGEMENT:

"Why are you downcast, O my soul? Why so disturbed within me? Put your hope in God, for I will yet praise him, my Savior and my God." Psalm 42:5

"Even youths grow tired and weary, and young men stumble and fall; but those who hope in the LORD will renew their strength." Isaiah 40:30-31

"For everything that was written in the past was written to teach us, so that through endurance and the encouragement of the Scriptures we might have hope." Romans 15:4

"Not only so, but we also rejoice in our sufferings, because we know that suffering produces perseverance; perseverance, character; and character, hope. And hope does not disappoint us, because God has poured out his love into our hearts by the Holy Spirit, whom he has given us." Romans 5:3-5

"For I know the plans I have for you," declares the LORD, "plans to prosper you and not harm you, plans to give you hope and a future. Then you will call upon me and come and pray to me, and I will listen to you. You will seek me and find me when you seek me with all your heart." Jeremiah 29:11-13

HOSPITALITY:

"Rather he must be hospitable, one who loves what is good, who is self-controlled, upright, holy and disciplined." Titus 1:8

"Share with God's people who are in need. Practice hospitality." Romans 12:13

"No widow may be put on the list of widows unless she is over sixty, has been faithful to her husband, and is well known for her good deeds, such as bringing up children, showing hospitality, washing the feet of the saints, helping those in trouble and devoting herself to all kinds of good deeds." 1 Timothy 5:9-10

"Offer hospitality to one another without grumbling." 1 Peter 4:9

JEALOUSY:

"But if you harbor bitter envy and selfish ambition in your hearts, do not boast about it or deny the truth. Such "wisdom" does not come down from heaven but is earthly, unspiritual, of the devil. For where you have envy and selfish ambition, there you find disorder and every evil practice." James 3:14-16

"You shall not covet you neighbor's house. You shall not covet your neighbor's wife, or his manservant or his maidservant, his ox or donkey, or anything that belongs to your neighbor." Exodus 20:17

"For the LORD your God is a consuming fire, a jealous God." Deuteronomy 4:24

"Do nothing out of selfish ambition or vain conceit, but in humility consider others better than yourselves." Philippians 2:3

JOY:

For seven days celebrate the Feast to the LORD your God at the place the LORD will choose. For the LORD your God will bless you in all your harvest and in all the work of your hands, and your joy will be complete." Deuteronomy 16:15

"Splendor and majesty are before him; strength and joy in his dwelling place." 1 Chronicles 16:27

"Be joyful always..." 1 Thessalonians 5:16

"For what is our hope, our joy, or the crown in which we will glory in the presence of our Lord Jesus when he comes? Is it not you? Indeed, you are our glory and joy." 1 Thessalonians 2:19-20

"Shout for joy to the LORD, all the earth. Worship the LORD with gladness; come before him with joyful songs." Psalm 100:1-2

LOVE:

"Love is patient, love is kind. It does not envy, it does not boast, it is not proud. It is not rude, it is not self-seeking, it is not easily angered, it keeps no record of wrongs. Love does not delight in evil but rejoices with the truth. It always protects, always trusts, always hopes, always perseveres." 1 Corinthians 13:4-7

"The trumpeters and musicians joined in unison to give praise and thanks to the Lord. Accompanied by trumpets, cymbals and other instruments, the singers raised their voices in praise to the Lord and sang: 'He is good; his love endures forever.' Then the temple of the Lord was filled with the cloud..." 2 Chronicles 5:13

"Your love, Lord, reaches to the heavens, your faithfulness to the skies." Psalm 36:5

"But I tell you: Love your enemies and pray for those who persecute you..." Matthew 5:44

"...'honor your father and your mother,' and 'love your neighbor as yourself.'" Matthew 19:19

"Instead, speaking the truth in love, we will in all things grow up into him who is the Head, that is, Christ." Ephesians 4:15

PARENTING (WISDOM FOR CHILDREN):

"She speaks with wisdom and faithful instruction is on her tongue." Proverbs 31:26

"Jesus said, 'Let the little children come to me and do not hinder them, for the kingdom of heaven belongs to such as these.'" Matthew 19:14

"Fathers, do not exasperate your children; instead, bring them up in the training and instruction of the LORD." Ephesians 6:4

"Only be careful, and watch yourselves closely so that you do not forget the things your eyes have seen or let them slip from your heart as long as you live. Teach them to your children and to their children after them." Deuteronomy 4:9

PATIENCE:

"A hot-tempered man stirs up dissension, but a patient man calms a quarrel." Proverbs 15:18

"And we urge you, brothers, warn those who are idle, encourage the timid, help the weak, be patient with everyone." 1 Thessalonians 5:14

"But if we hope for what we do not yet have, we wait for it patiently." Romans 8:25

"A man's wisdom gives him patience, it is to his glory to overlook an offense." Proverbs 19:11

PEACE/CONTENTMENT:

"Turn from evil and do good; seek peace and pursue it." Psalm 34:14

"Blessed are the peacemakers, for they will be called sons of God." Matthew 5:9

"A heart of peace gives life to the body, but envy rots the bones." Proverbs 14:30

"I am not saying this because I am in need, for I have learned to be content whatever the circumstances." Philippians 4:11

"Peace I leave with you; my peace I give you. I do not give to you as the world gives. Do not let your hearts be troubled and do not be afraid." John 14:27

"Keep your lives free from the love of money and be content with what you have, because God has said, 'Never will I leave you; never will I forsake you.'" Hebrews 13:5

PERSEVERANCE:

"As you know, we consider blessed those who have persevered. You have heard of Job's perseverance and have seen what the Lord finally brought about. The Lord is full of compassion and mercy." James 5:11

"Blessed is the man who perseveres under trial, because when he has stood the test, he will receive the crown of life that God has promised to those who love him." James 1:12

"Therefore, since we are surrounded by such a great cloud of witnesses, let us throw off everything that hinders and the sin that so easily entangles, and let us run with perseverance the race marked out for us." Hebrews 12:1

"Watch your life and doctrine closely. Persevere in them, because if you do, you will save both yourself and your hearers." 1 Timothy 4:16

PURPOSE:

"For we are God's workmanship, created in Christ Jesus to do good works, which God prepared in advance for us to do." Ephesians 2:10

"But in fact God has arranged the parts in the body, every one of them, just as he wanted them to be. If they were all one part, where would the body be? As it is, there are many parts, but one body...Now you are the body of Christ, and each one of you is a part of it." 1 Corinthians 12:18-20, 27

"We have different gifts, according to the grace given us. If a man's gift is prophesying, let him use it in proportion to his faith. If it is serving, let him serve; if it is teaching, let him teach; if it is encouraging, then let him encourage; if it is contributing to the needs of others, let him give generously; if it is leadership, let him govern diligently; if it is showing mercy, let him do it cheerfully." Romans 12:6-8

"For you created my inmost being; you knit me together in my mother's womb. I praise you because I am fearfully and wonderfully made, I know that full well...All the days ordained for me were written in your book before one of them came to be." Psalm 139:13-14, 16b

REST:

"By the seventh day God had finished the work he had been doing; so on the seventh day he rested from all his work. And God blessed the seventh day and made it holy, because on it he rested from all the work of creating that he had done." Genesis 2:2-3

"Remember the Sabbath day by keeping it holy. Six days you shall labor and do all your work, but the seventh day is a Sabbath to the LORD your God. On it you shall not do any work, neither you, nor your son or daughter, nor your manservant or maidservant, nor your animals, nor the alien within your gates." Exodus 20:8-10

"A man can do nothing better than to eat and drink and find satisfaction in his work. This too, I see, is from the hand of God, for without him, who can eat or find enjoyment?" Ecclesiastes 2:24-25

"Come to me, all you who are weary and burdened, and I will give you rest. Take my yoke upon you and learn from me, for I am gentle and humble in heart, and you will find rest for your souls. For my yoke is easy and my burden is light." Matthew 11:28-30

"Then, because so many people were coming and going that they did not even have a chance to eat, he said to them, 'Come with me by yourselves to a quiet place and get some rest.'" Mark 6:31

SAFETY/PROTECTION:

"He who dwells in the shelter of the Most High, will rest in the shadow of the Almighty. I will say of the LORD, 'He is my refuge and my fortress, my God in whom I trust.' Surely he will save you from the fowler's snare and from the deadly pestilence." Psalm 91:1-3

Scriptures To Study For Bible Studies And Personal Devotionals

"The LORD will keep you from all harm-he will watch over your life; the LORD will watch over your coming and going both now and forevermore." Psalm 121:7-8

"The name of the LORD is a strong tower; the righteous run to it and are safe." Proverbs 18:10

"For he will command his angels concerning you to guard you in all your ways..." Psalm 91:11

SALVATION:

"In that day they will say, 'Surely this is our God; we trusted in him, and he saved us. This is the LORD, we trusted in him; let us rejoice and be glad in his salvation.'" Isaiah 25:9

"Salvation is found in no one else, for there is no other name (Jesus) under heaven given to men by which we must be saved." Acts 4:12

"The LORD is my strength and my song; he has become my salvation." Exodus 15:2a

"The LORD is my light and my salvation-whom shall I fear? The LORD is the stronghold of my life-of whom shall I be afraid?" Psalm 27:1

"...That if you confess with your mouth, 'Jesus is Lord,' and believe in your heart that God raised him from the dead, you will be saved." Romans 10:9

"On hearing this, Jesus said to them, 'It is not the healthy who need a doctor, but the sick. I have not come to call the righteous, but sinners.'" Mark 2:17

"Repent, then, and turn to God, so that your sins may be wiped out, that times of refreshing may come from the Lord..." Acts 3:19

"For God so loved the world that he gave his one and only Son, that whoever believes in him shall not perish but have eternal life." John 3:16

SERVING:

"But be sure to fear the LORD and serve him faithfully with all your heart; consider what great things he has done for you." 1 Samuel 12:24

"Serve wholeheartedly, as if you were serving the Lord, not men..." Ephesians 6:7

"There are different kinds of service, but the same Lord." 1 Corinthians 12:5

"But if serving the LORD seems undesirable to you, then choose for yourselves this day whom you will serve, whether the gods your forefathers served beyond the River, or the gods of the Amorites, in whose land you are living. But as for me and my household, we will serve the LORD." Joshua 24:15

"Search me, O God, and know my heart; test me and know my anxious thoughts. See if there is any offensive way in me, and lead me in the way everlasting." Psalm 139:23-24

ABOUT THE AUTHOR

Lisa D. Weitkamp lives in mid-Missouri with her husband Danny, their four children-Hunter. Colt, D.J., and Autumn-and their two dogs, Oscar and Tuffy. She enjoys reading, spending time with family, and going on new adventures, such as zip lining and visiting historical places.

As a new author, Lisa has published numerous devotionals for church and has a Facebook page titled: Lisa Weitkamp-Author.

With her God-given gift of writing, Lisa hopes to inspire others and to help them understand the depth of the Father's love. She wants to continue her career as an author so keep watching for more books in the future!

Dear Ross and Taylor,

Congratulations on being new parents! The adventure will have its ups and downs. Even so, raising your own child is very rewarding. Always remember to seek God and He'll help you along the way. That's what I've learned so far. I hope you enjoy the book and your precious new baby.

God bless!
Lisa & Family

9 781498 479967